GUITAR
CHORD BOOK

Publications
International, Ltd.

Contents

CHORDS WITH BIG PAYOFFS

There are plenty of guitar chords to be learned—thousands, in fact. But you don't need to know thousands of chords to play a lot of songs. In fact, you only need to know a handful. The chords in this book are the ones you'll discover in all of today's major genres, including rock, pop, R&B, country, and jazz.

While there are many variations on the finger patterns and positions for every chord, we supply you with the basic ones to get you started. They're the workhorses of common chord progressions and they'll pay off quickly!

he acoustic guitar is a portable instrument that you can play
nywhere without worrying about amplifiers or microphones.
But while it may have started out as an instrument common
o intimate settings like coffeehouses and campfires, the
coustic guitar has benefited from contemporary pick-up
echnology. From the garage to the arena, the acoustic can
jo anywhere the electric goes.

n the 1920s jazz musicians amplified their archtop acoustic guitars
with microphone-type pick-ups. These guitars were forerunners
o the modern solid body electric guitar we know today. In the
1940s a musician named Les Paul developed the solid body
guitar by using a solid piece of wood for the body of the guitar.
This gave the guitar more sustain and less feedback when played
at higher volumes.

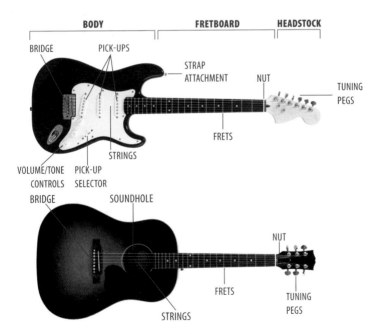

E string ——
A string ——
D string ——
G string ——
B string ——
E string ——

The diameter of a string—its gauge—is measured in centimeters: the lower numbers designate the thinner strings. Electric guitar players prefer light gauge strings (0.09–0.42) because they are easier to bend. Acoustic strings are heavier. They range from 0.10–0.47 (light) to 0.13–0.57 (heavy). The style of playing often determines the string size the player uses. For example, a finger-style player might use a lighter gauge string while a blues or slide player would prefer a heavy string.

Once you have played guitar for a while you may want to experiment with different strings. Once you settle on a style of playing you usually settle on a particular type of string.

Strings have changed over the years. Manufacturers still try different alloys or types of windings. A recent addition is the coated string—this string has a thin layer of plastic that keeps it free from oil and dirt, and gives the player a better-sounding, longer-lasting string.

Classical guitar players use a different type of string. Their instruments can't support a high amount of tension on the neck, so they use a special nylon string that doesn't require the tight winding of a steel string.

PLAY FROM THE GUT?

Steel guitar strings are a relatively new invention. So before steel, nylon, and other synthetic materials, what did musicians use to string their guitars? Three common materials were hair, animal gut (yes, intestines from animals like sheep and cows), and silk.

TUNING PEGS & NUT

A guitar has six *tuning pegs* that may be positioned on one side of the headstock or three to a side.

The strings are laid over small grooves on the *nut*. This holds them in place.

FRET MARKERS

On the side of the guitar neck are tiny dots called *fret markers*. Often there will be two dots on the twelfth fret.

THE BRIDGE

The strings travel down the neck and go over the *bridge*. On most acoustic guitars the strings are anchored through the bridge with bridge pins. On electric guitars, strings may be fastened to the bridge, the tailpiece, or be run through the body of the guitar itself.

VOLUME/TONE CONTROLS & PICK-UP SELECTOR

Electric guitars and some acoustic guitars are equipped with *volume* and *tone controls*. On the electric guitars that have more than one pick-up there is a *pick-up selector*. On a Les Paul-type guitar it is located on the upper left side of the body. On a Fender-type guitar it is located near the volume/tone controls.

Hand and Finger Position

THE GUITAR PICK

old the pick firmly in its larger section.
e sure the pick is at a ninety-degree
ngle to the guitar and strum from the
op string to the bottom string. Your
rist should be loose enough to strum
p and down on all the strings.

USING YOUR LEFT HAND

Your left hand holds the notes down. The most important part of guitar playing involves the left hand.

Let's start with numbering the left hand. When you are trying new chords, there are times that your fingers don't actually move to the right position. Try using your other hand to push the finger that doesn't quite fit into position.

When you wrap your left-hand fingers around the fretboard, make sure that you arch your hand so that your thumb is perpendicular and directly behind the neck.

Southpaw Blues

The instructions and images in this book reference right-handed playing techniques and positions. If you are playing a left-handed guitar, hand and finger positions will appear reversed.

Holding Your Guitar

There are many ways to hold a guitar while playing, but keep these tips in mind to make it more comfortable to play.

When standing or sitting make sure that your arms are loose and not holding up any of the weight of the guitar. Always keep the neck of the guitar aimed up slightly. Don't point it at the floor. Use a strap when standing. Adjust it until it feels comfortable. Make sure your left arm is not overextended and your fingers can easily reach all the positions on the fretboard. You will notice some players prefer a "low-slung" guitar. This style is for "looks," and doesn't help you play well.

When sitting, you might find it comfortable to cross your legs. This raises the guitar for easier playing. Some players, especially classical guitarists, use a footstool and rest the guitar on the right thigh.

Know Your Notes

...ere is a simple logic to the arrangement of notes on ...e fretboard. Let's look at each string to see how the ...etboard works, starting from the lowest note—the ...en E on the top E string.

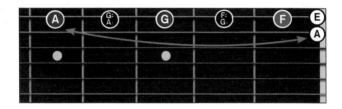

...eginning with open E, play the first six notes. They ...re E, F, F#/Gb, G, G#/Ab, and A. Now play the open ... on the next string. If you have tuned your guitar ...orrectly, the A on the E string and the open A should ...ound the same. This is the beginning of a pattern on ...he fretboard.

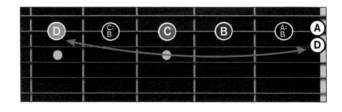

Beginning with open A, play the first six notes. Then play the open D on the next string. As with the two A notes, the two D notes should sound the same.

11

On the E, A, D, and B strings, the fifth fretted note is the same as the open note on the next string. On the G string, you only up four frets.

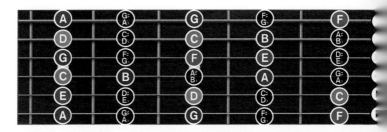

Chords

Put simply, chords are made when you play two or more notes at the same time. The most common, a *triad*, is when three notes are combined. A triad is the superposition of two thirds. The notes are named the *root*, *third*, and *fifth*. The triad shown here is from the C major scale. It consists of the notes C, E, and G.

fifth
third
root

u may be surprised to learn that chords have personalities.
nen you listen to a song and identify it with a mood—gloomy,
lifting, jarring, or dreamy—you are reacting to the power of
e song's chords. If you want to start an argument between two
ngwriters, ask them what gives chords their different moods.
e debate is ongoing, but here are a few common opinions:

A chord is simply a combination of pitches. We've been
earing these combinations since childhood and have been
onditioned to associate them with different emotions.
other words, it's cultural.

Chords tap into innate biological preferences. Our ears
aturally hear some intervals within chords as consonant
armonious or settled) and others as dissonant. We assign
oods to chords based on their relative consonance
r dissonance.

It depends on the company a chord keeps. A single
ninor chord in a progression of major chords may be very
oothing. Group that chord with other minor chords and it
nay sound melancholy.

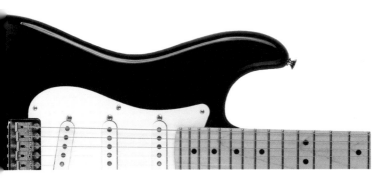

In the 1940s, songwriter and guitarist Les Paul crafted a new kind of electric guitar. It featured two pickups and a solid wooden body. (In fact, he called it "The Log" because it was made from thick railroad timber). Les Paul's invention caught on with other guitarists—and thousands of models and innovations followed.

The Telecaster

In the early 1950s, the first solid-body electric guitar was introduced commercially. The Telecaster is simple in design, featuring a one-piece body, a bolt-on neck, and two pickups controlled by a three-position selector. There is one volume and one tone control.

The Les Paul

First produced in 1952, this solid-body electric guitar has remained virtually unchanged for over half a century. Its thick, heavy body gives it a thick tone with notable sustain.

The Stratocaster

top-seller since 1954, the iconic Stratocaster is simply designed t amazingly versatile in tone. Its three single coil pickups provide itarists with a broad tonal palette.

The ES-335

ne ES-335 was first manufactured in 1958. An electric uitar with a hollow body, this semi-acoustic instrument rovides a great palette of sounds, from warm and mellow zzy tones to bright, soaring leads. A solid block of wood eneath the pickups reduces feedback problems associated vith semi-acoustic guitars.

The SG

Gibson introduced the SG in 1961. It's a no-frills guitar great for playing rock 'n' roll. The double-cutaway design allows easy access to the highest frets.

C Major

1st position

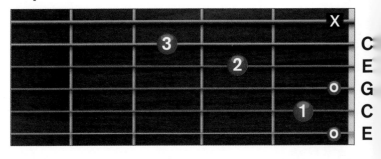

C Major

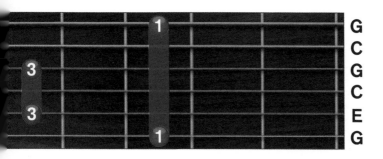

G
C
G
C
E
G

Fret 5

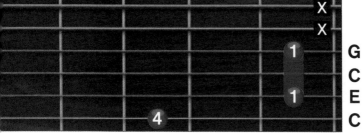

G
C
E
C

Csus4

C Suspended 4th

1st position

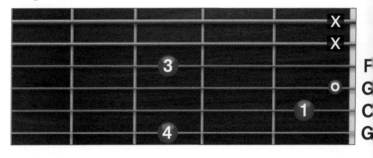

F
G
C
G

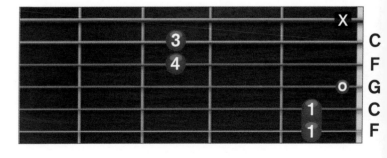

C
F
G
C
F

18

Csus4

C Suspended 4th

Fret 3

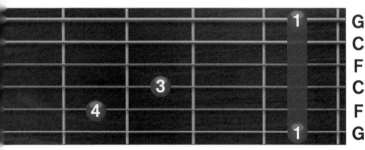

G
C
F
C
F
G

Fret 5

G
C
F
C

C Major 6th

1st position

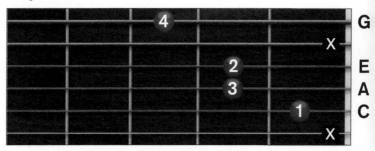

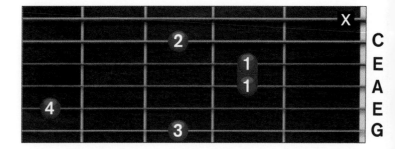

C Major 6th

Fret 3

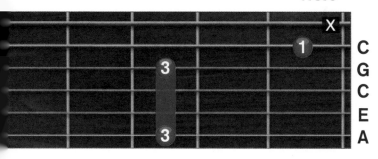

C
G
C
E
A

Fret 5

E
A
C
G

C Major 6th add 9th

1st position

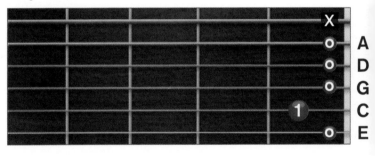

A
D
G
C
E

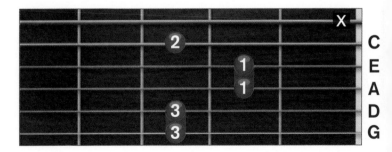

C
E
A
D
G

C Major 6th add 9th

Fret 5

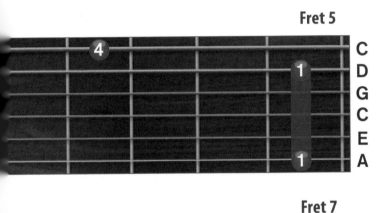

C
D G
C E A

Fret 7

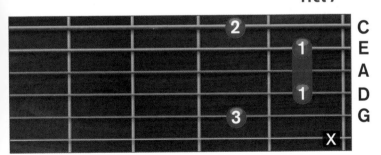

C
E A D G

Cmaj7

C Major 7th

1st position

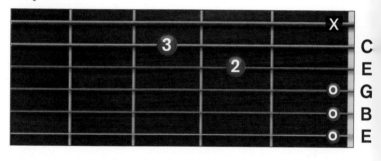

C
E
G o
B o
E o

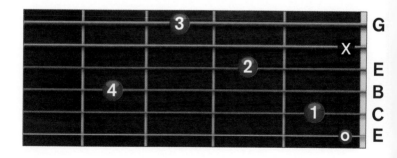

G
X
E
B
C
E o

24

Cmaj7
C Major 7th

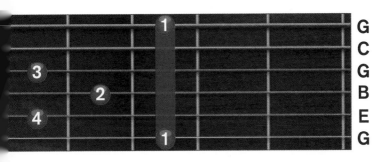

G
C
G
B
E
G

Fret 7

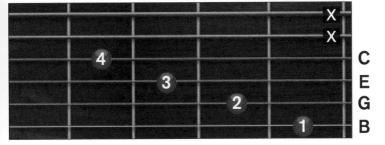

X
X
C
E
G
B

25

C Minor

1st position

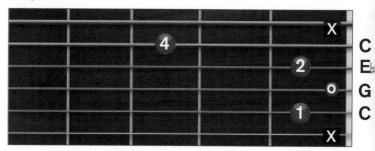

C
E♭
G
C

Fret 3

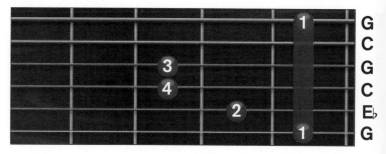

G
C
G
C
E♭
G

26

C Minor

Fret 4

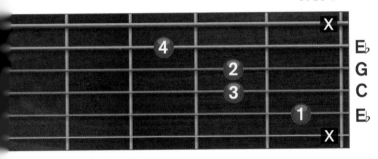

E♭
G
C
E♭

Fret 5

G
E♭
G
C

C Minor 6th

1st position

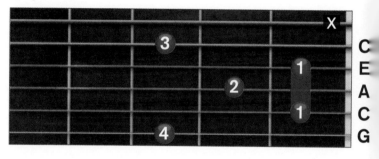

C
E
A
C
G

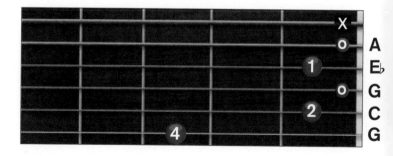

A
E♭
G
C
G

28

Cm6

C Minor 6th

Fret 3

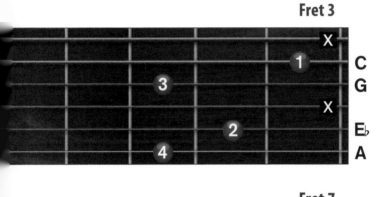

X
C
G
X
E♭
A

Fret 7

C
X
A
E♭
G
X

C Minor 7th

1st position

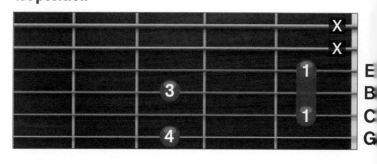

E
B
C
G

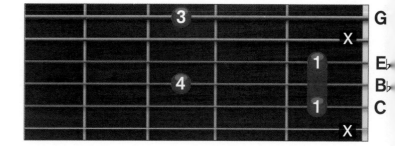

G
X
E♭
B♭
C
X

C Minor 7th

Fret 3

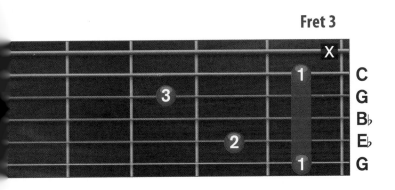

X
C
G
B♭
E♭
G

Fret 7

C
X
B♭
E♭
G
X

C Dominant 7th

1st position

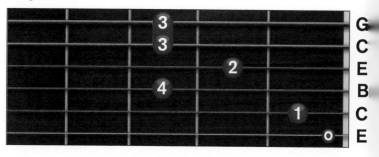

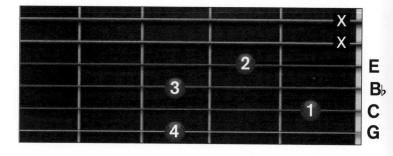

C Dominant 7th

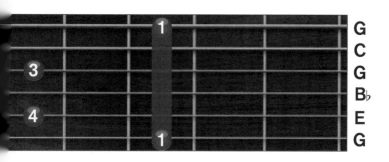

G
C
G
B♭
E
G

Fret 3

X
C
G
C
E
B♭

C Dominant 9th

1st position

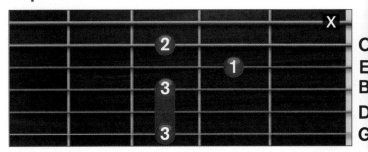

C
E
B
D
G

Fret 5

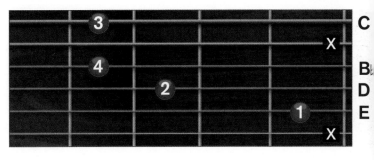

C
B♭
D
E

34

C Dominant 9th

Fret 7

E
B♭
D
G
C

Fret 7

C
E
B♭
D

C# Major

1st position

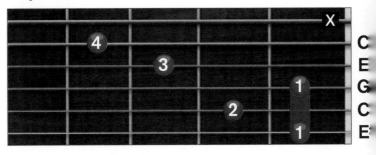

C
E
G
C
E

G#
E#
G#
C#

36

C# Major

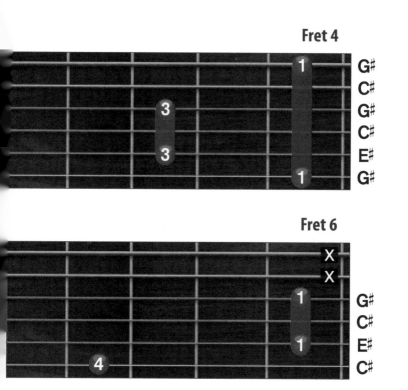

Fret 4

1 — G#
— C#
3 — G#
— C#
3 — E#
1 — G#

Fret 6

X
X
1 — G#
— C#
1 — E#
4 — C#

37

C#sus4

C# Suspended 4th

1st position

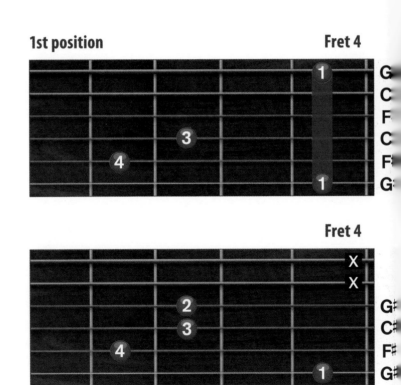

Fret 4

G#
C#
F#
C#
F#
G#

Fret 4

X
X
G#
C#
F#
G#

38

C# Suspended 4th

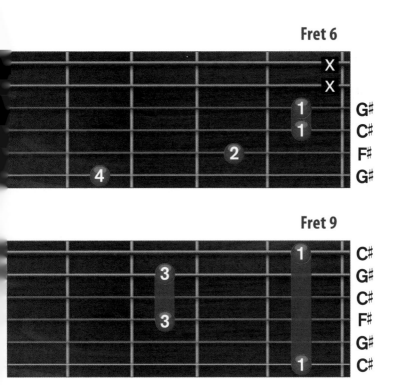

Fret 6

X
X
1 — G#
1 — C#
2 — F#
4 — G#

Fret 9

1 — C#
3 — G#
3 — C#
F#
G#
1 — C#

39

C# Major 6th

1st position

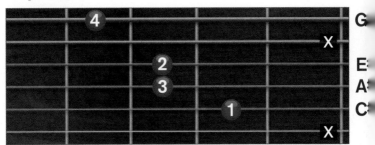

G
X
E#
A#
C#

X
X
E#
A#
C#
G#

C# Major 6th

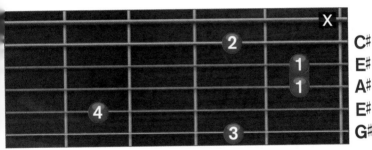

Fret 3

C#
E#
A#
E#
G#

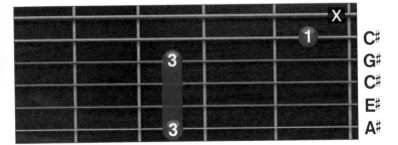

Fret 4

C#
G#
C#
E#
A#

41

C♯ Major 6th add 9th

1st position

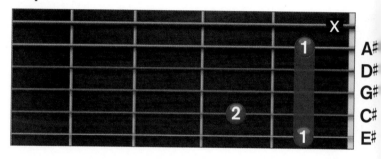

A♯
D♯
G♯
C♯
E♯

Fret 3

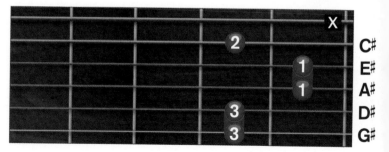

C♯
E♯
A♯
D♯
G♯

42

C# Major 6th add 9th

Fret 6

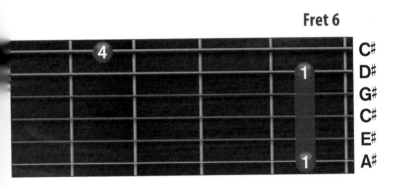

C#
D#
G#
C#
E#
A#

Fret 8

C#
E#
A#
D#
G#
C#

43

C#maj7

C# Major 7th

1st position

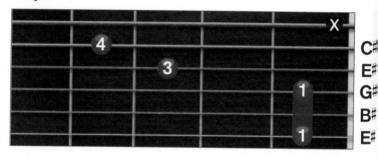

C#
E#
G#
B#
E#

G#

E#
B#
C#

44

C#maj7

C# Major 7th

Fret 4

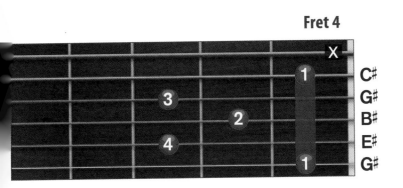

C#
G#
B#
E#
G#

Fret 6

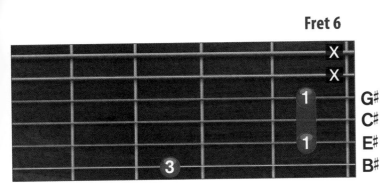

G#
C#
E#
B#

45

C# Minor

1st position

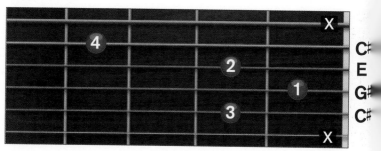

C#
E
G#
C#

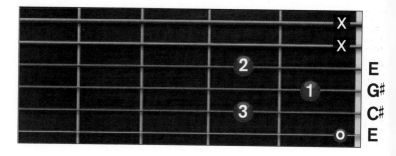

E
G#
C#
E

C# Minor

Fret 4

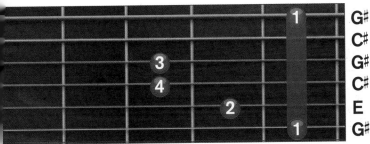

G#
C#
G#
C#
E
G#

Fret 6

E
G#
C#
G#

47

C♯ Minor 6th

1st position

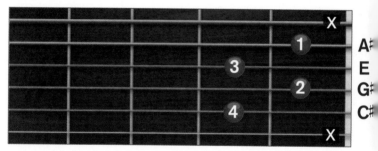

A♯
E
G♯
C♯

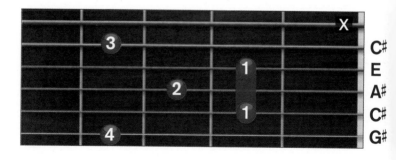

C♯
E
A♯
C♯
G♯

48

C# Minor 6th

Fret 3

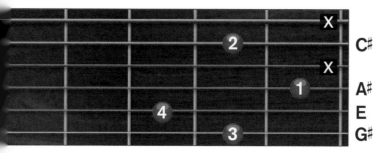

X
C#
X
A#
E
G#

Fret 4

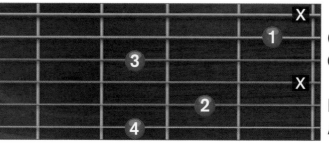

X
C#
G#
X
E
A#

49

C♯ Minor 7th

1st position

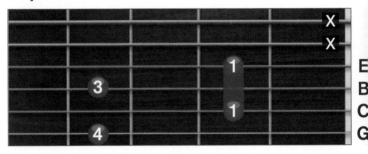

50

C# Minor 7th

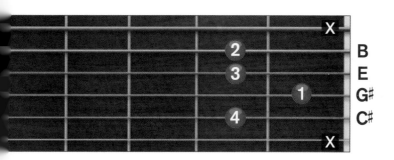

B
E
G#
C#

Fret 4

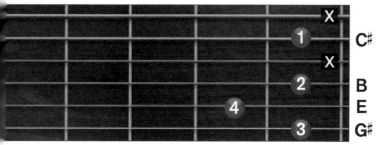

C#

B
E
G#

51

C♯ Dominant 7th

1st position

G
C
E
B
C
X

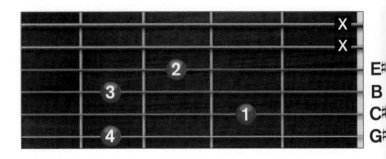

X
X
E♯
B
C♯
G♯

C# Dominant 7th

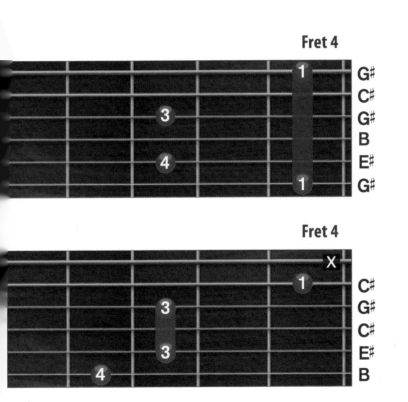

Fret 4

G#
C#
G#
B
E#
G#

Fret 4

C#
G#
C#
E#
B

C♯ Dominant 9th

1st position

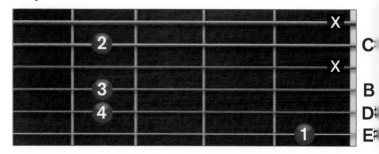

C♯
B
D♯
E♯

Fret 3

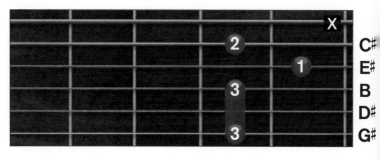

C♯
E♯
B
D♯
G♯

54

C# Dominant 9th

Fret 6

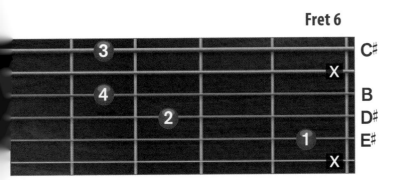

C#
X
B
D#
E#
X

Fret 8

C#
E#
B
D#
X
X

D Major

1st position

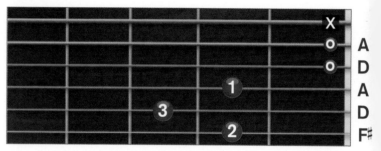

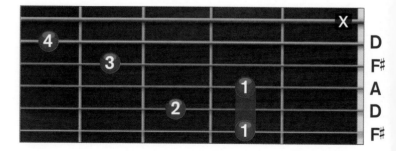

56

D Major

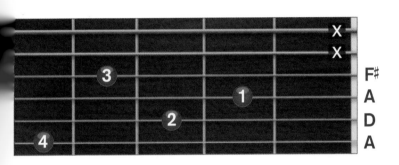

F#
A
D
D
A

Fret 5

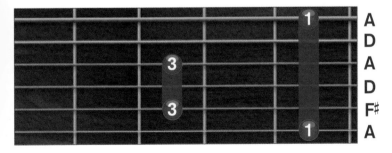

A
D
A
D
F#
A

D Suspended 4th

1st position

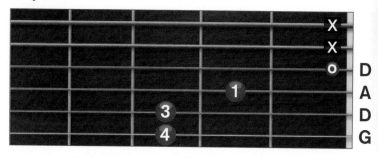

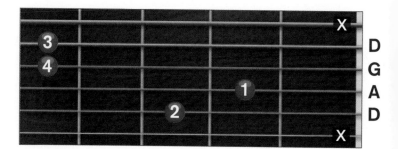

Dsus4

D Suspended 4th

Fret 5

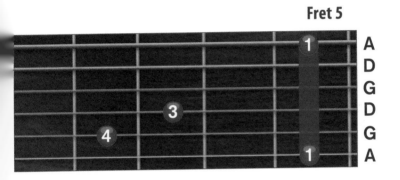

A
D
G
D
G
A

Fret 7

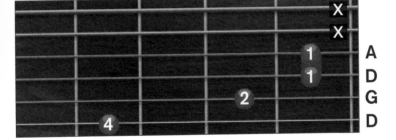

A
D
G
D

D Major 6th

1st position

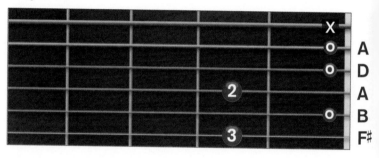

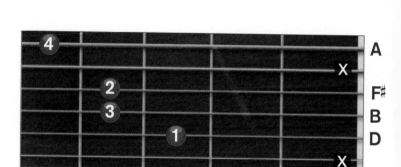

D Major 6th

Fret 5

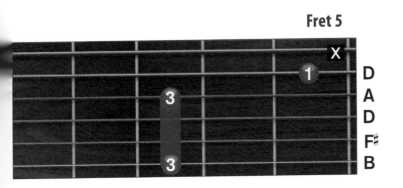

D
A
D
F#
B

Fret 9

D

B
F#
A

61

D Major 6th add 9th

1st position

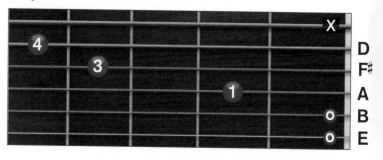

D
F#
A
B
E

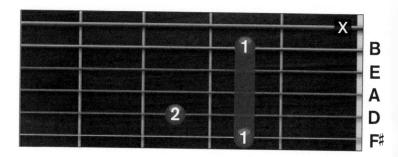

B
E
A
D
F#

D Major 6th add 9th

Fret 4

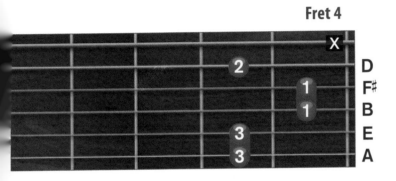

D
F#
B
E
A

Fret 7

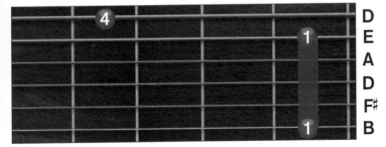

D
E
A
D
F#
B

Dmaj7

D Major 7th

1st position

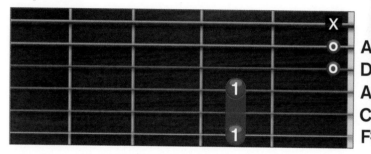

X
A
A
D
A
C#
F#

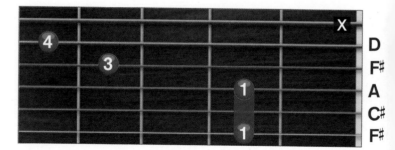

X
D
F#
A
C#
F#

D Major 7th

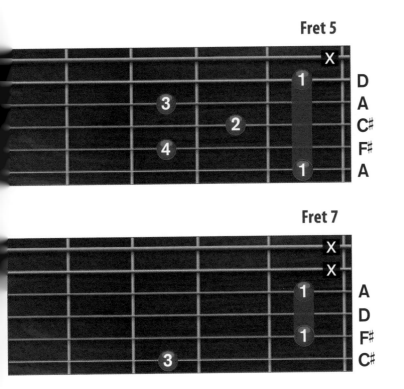

Fret 5

X
1 — D
3
A
2 — C#
4
F#
1 — A

Fret 7

X
X
1 — A
D
1 — F#
3
C#

65

D Minor

1st position

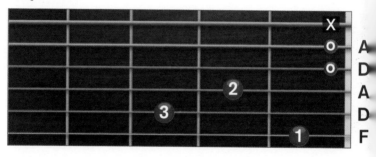

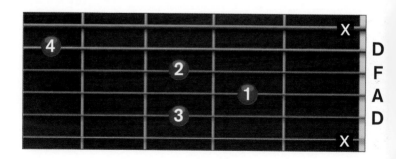

66

D Minor

Fret 5

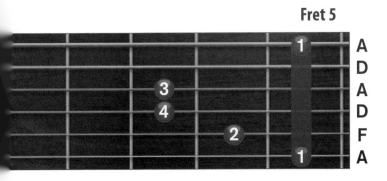

A
D
A
D
F
A

Fret 7

X
F
A
D
A
X

Dm6

D Minor 6th

1st position

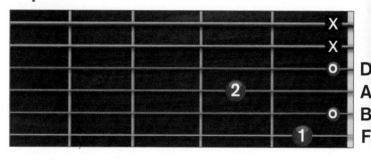

D Minor 6th

Fret 3

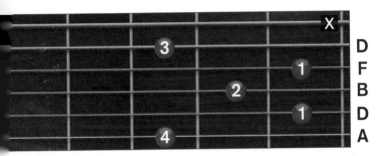

X
D
F
B
D
A

Fret 5

X
D
A
X
F
B

D Minor 7th

1st position

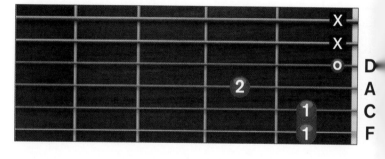

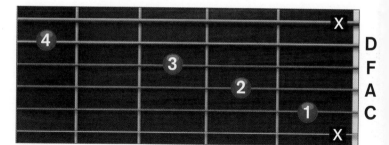

D Minor 7th

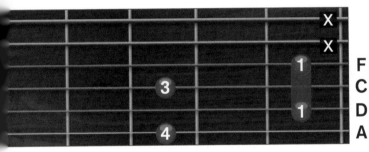

X
X
F
C
D
A

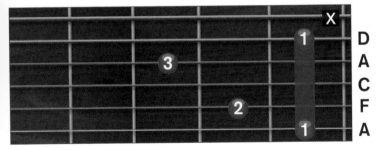

X
D
A
C
F
A

D Dominant 7th

1st position

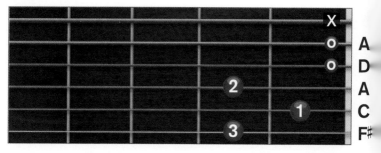

Fret 3

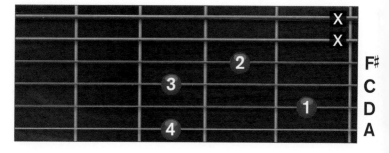

72

D Dominant 7th

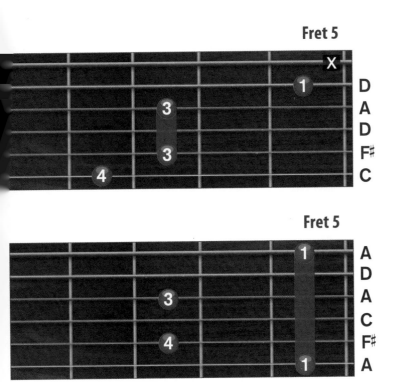

Fret 5

D
A
D
F#
C

Fret 5

A
D
A
C
F#
A

D Dominant 9th

1st position

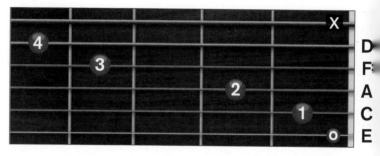

D
F#
A
C
E

Fret 4

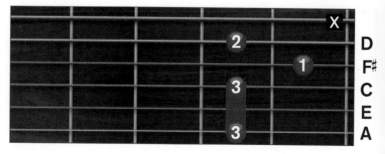

D
F#
C
E
A

74

D Dominant 9th

Fret 7

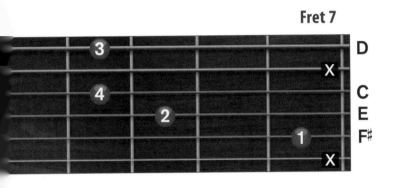

D
X
C
E
F♯
X

Fret 9

D
F♯
C
E
X
X

75

E♭ Major

1st position

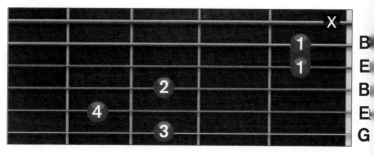

B
E
B♭
E♭
G

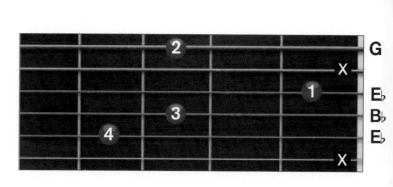

G
X
E♭
B♭
E♭
X

76

E♭ Major

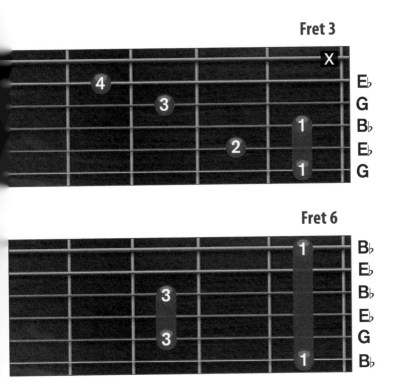

Fret 3

X
E♭
G
B♭
E♭
G

Fret 6

B♭
E♭
B♭
E♭
G
B♭

Eb Suspended 4th

1st position

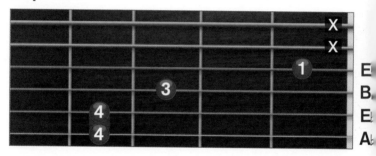

E
Bb
Eb
Ab

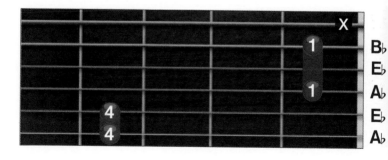

Bb
Eb
Ab
Eb
Ab

78

E♭ Suspended 4th

Fret 3

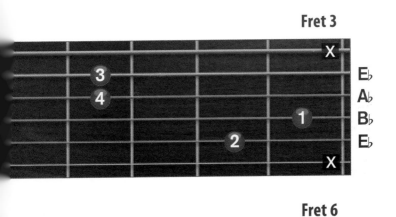

E♭
A♭
B♭
E♭

Fret 6

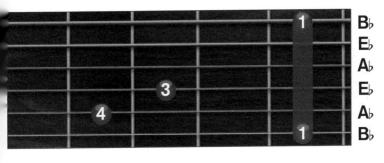

B♭
E♭
A♭
E♭
A♭
B♭

Eb Major 6th

1st position

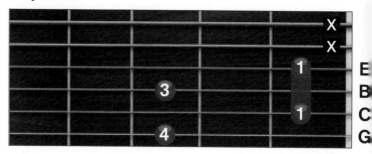

E
B
C
G

Fret 4

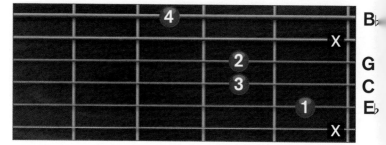

Bb
G
C
Eb

80

E♭ Major 6th

Fret 5

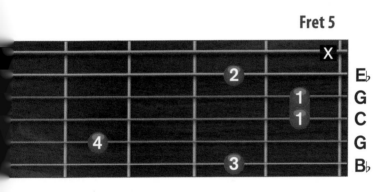

X

E♭
G
C
G
B♭

Fret 6

X

E♭
B♭
E♭
G
C

Eb 6th add 9th

1st position

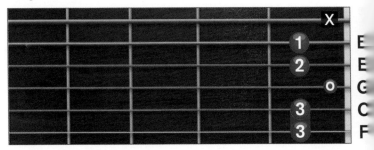

E
E
G
C
F

Fret 3

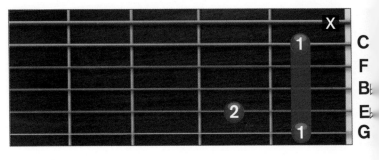

C
F
Bb
Eb
G

82

E♭ 6th add 9th

Fret 5

E♭
G
C
F
B♭

Fret 8

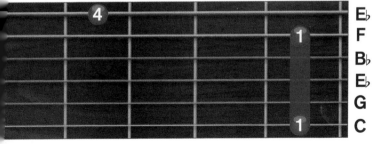

E♭
F
B♭
E♭
G
C

E♭ Major 7th

1st position

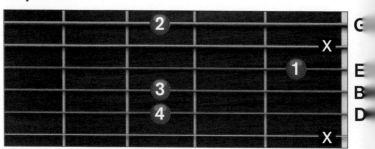

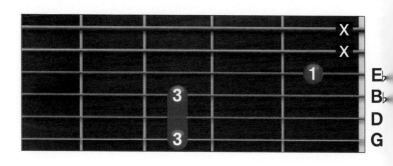

84

E♭ Major 7th

Fret 3

E♭
G
B♭
D
G

Fret 6

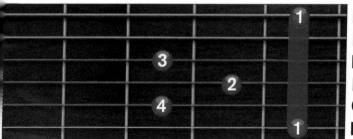

B♭
E♭
B♭
D
G
B♭

E♭ Minor

1st position

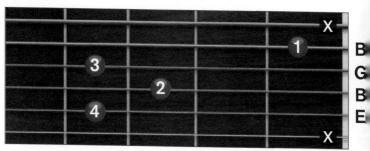

Eb Minor

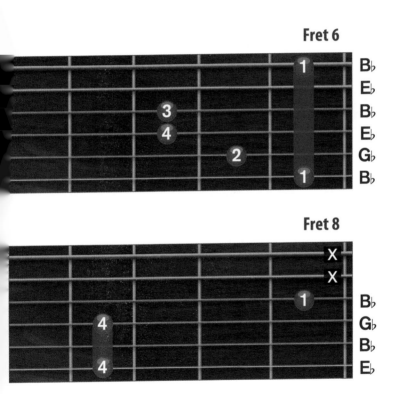

Fret 6

Bb
Eb
Bb
Eb
Gb
Bb

Fret 8

Bb
Gb
Bb
Eb

Eb Minor 6th

1st position

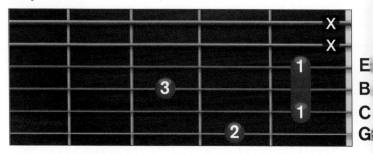

E♭ Minor 6th

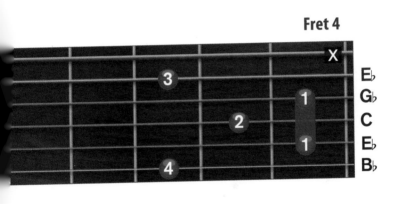

Fret 4

E♭
G♭
C
E♭
B♭

Fret 6

E♭
B♭

G♭
C

Eb Minor 7th

1st position

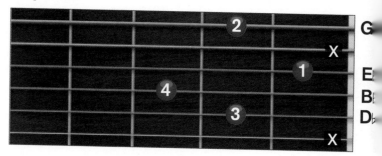

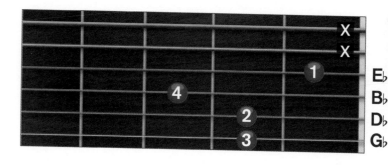

90

E♭m7

E♭ Minor 7th

Fret 4

E♭
G♭
D♭
E♭
B♭

Fret 6

E♭
B♭
D♭
G♭
B♭

E♭ Dominant 7th

1st position

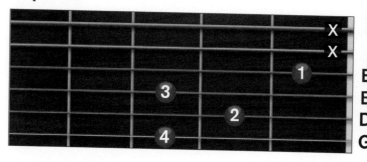

E♭ Dominant 7th

Fret 4

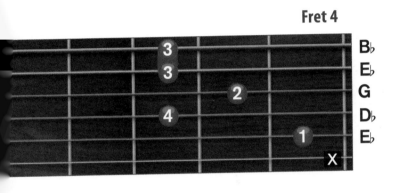

B♭
E♭
G
D♭
E♭
X

Fret 6

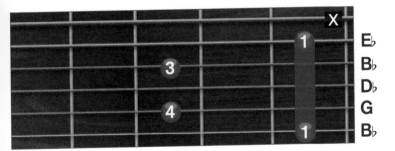

X
E♭
B♭
D♭
G
B♭

E♭ Dominant 9th

1st position

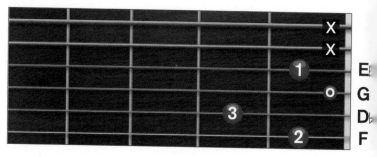

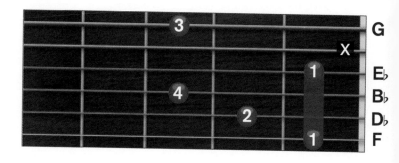

94

Eb Dominant 9th

Fret 3

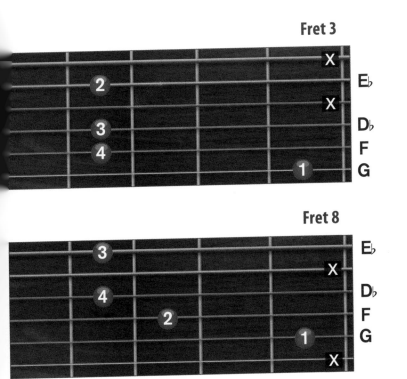

Eb
Db
F
G

Fret 8

Eb
Db
F
G

E Major

1st position

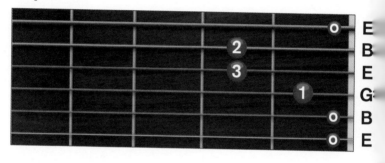

E
E B
E G
E G♯
B
E

E
E B
E E
E B
E E
G♯

E Major

Fret 4

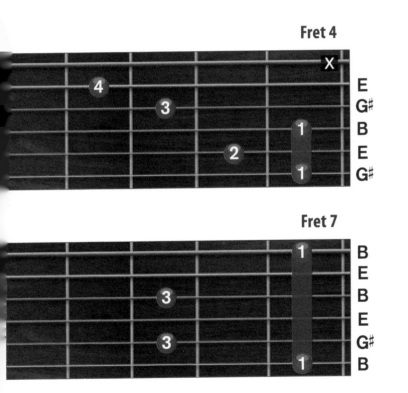

X

E
G#
B
E
G#

Fret 7

B
E
B
E
G#
B

E Suspended 4th

1st position

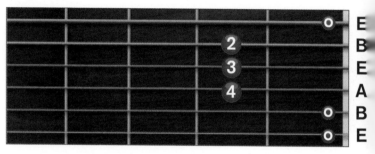

Esus4

E Suspended 4th

Fret 4

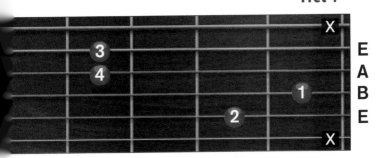

E
A
B
E

Fret 7

B
E
A
E
A
B

E Major 6th

1st position

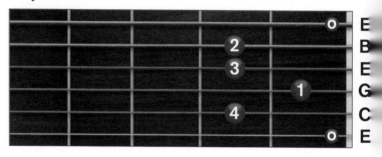

E Major 6th

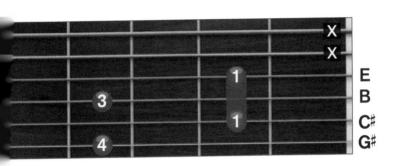

E
B
C#
G#

Fret 6

E
C#
G#
B

E Major 6th add 9th

1st position

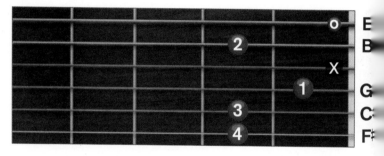

E
B
G
C#
F#

Fret 6

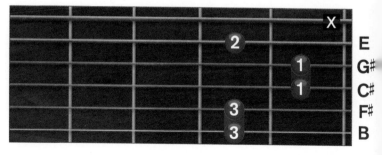

E
G#
C#
F#
B

E Major 6th add 9th

Fret 9

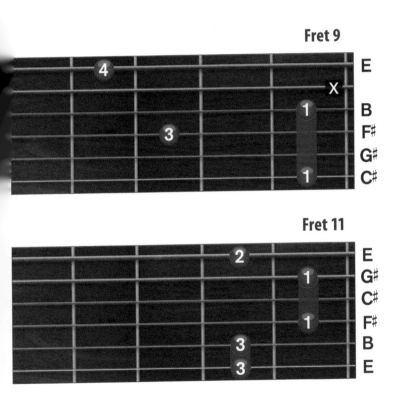

Fret 9 (top diagram):
- 4
- X
- 1 — B
- 3 — F#
- G#
- 1 — C#
- E

Fret 11

Fret 11 (bottom diagram):
- 2 — E
- 1 — G#
- C#
- 1 — F#
- 3 — B
- 3 — E

E Major 7th

1st position

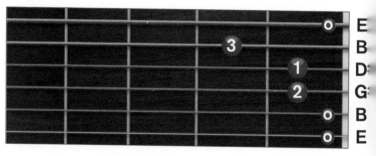

E
B
D#
G#
B
E

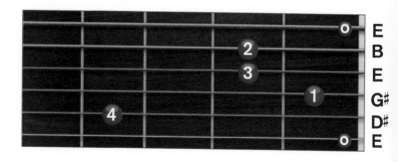

E
B
E
G#
D#
E

104

E Major 7th

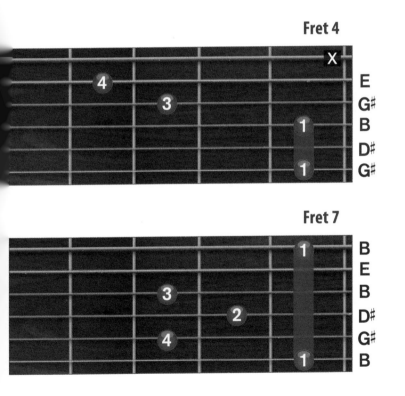

Fret 4

X

E
G#
B
D#
G#

Fret 7

B
E
B
D#
G#
B

105

E Minor

1st position

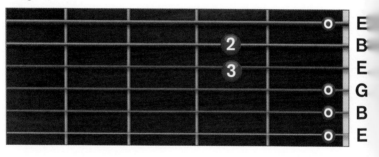

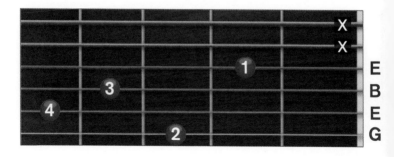

E Minor

Fret 4

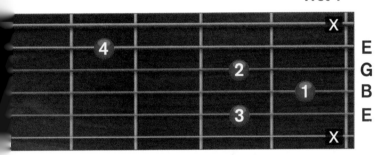

E
G
B
E

Fret 7

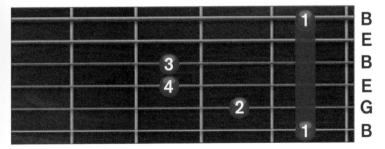

B
E
B
E
G
B

E Minor 6th

1st position

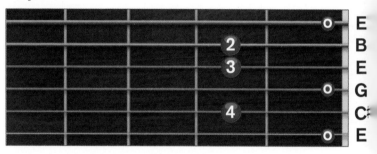

E Minor 6th

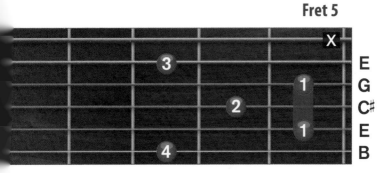

Fret 5

E
G
C#
E
B

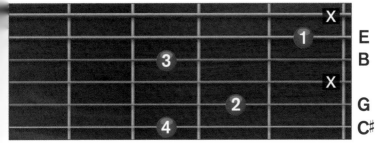

Fret 7

E
B

G
C#

E Minor 7th

1st position

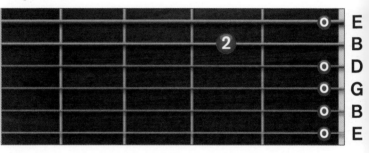

E Minor 7th

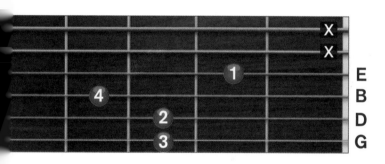

E
B
D
G

Fret 5

E
G
D
E
B

111

E Dominant 7th

1st position

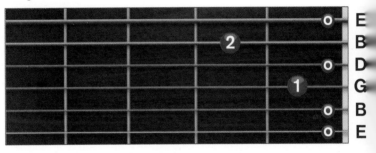

E Dominant 7th

Fret 5

B
E
G#
D
E
X

Fret 7

B
E
B
D
G#
B

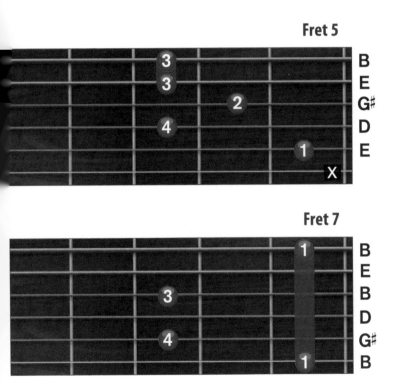

113

E Dominant 9th

1st position

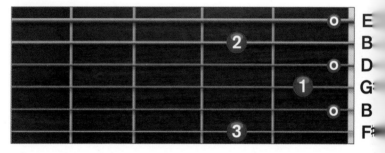

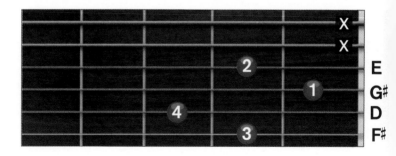

E Dominant 9th

Fret 4

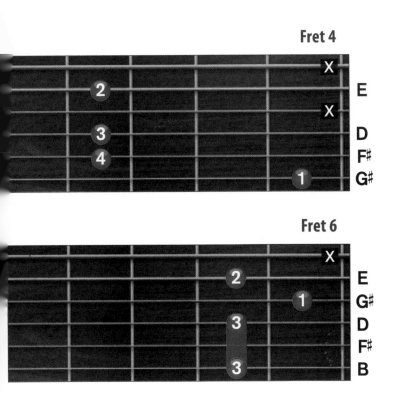

X
E
X
D
F#
G#

Fret 6

X
E
G#
D
F#
B

F Major

1st position

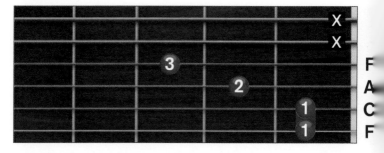

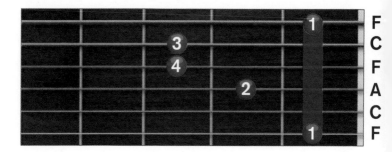

116

F Major

Fret 5

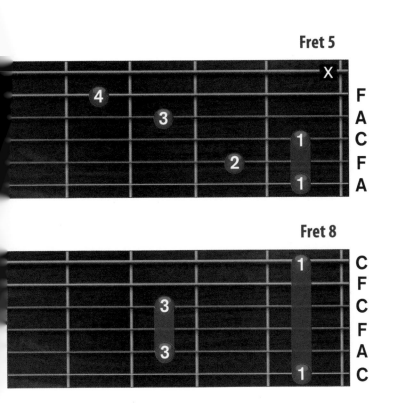

F Suspended 4th

1st position

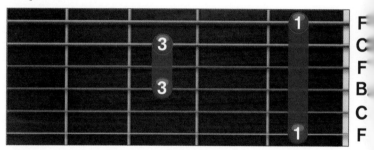

F
C
F
B♭
C
F

Fret 3

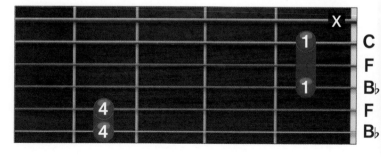

C
F
B♭
F
B♭

F Suspended 4th

Fret 3

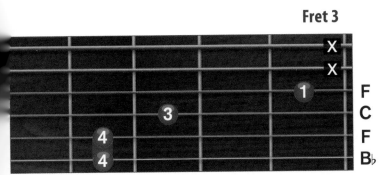

F
C
F
B♭

Fret 8

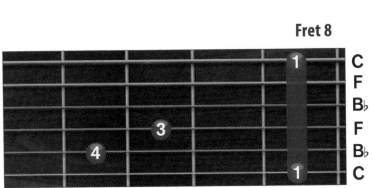

C
F
B♭
F
B♭
C

F Major 6th

1st position

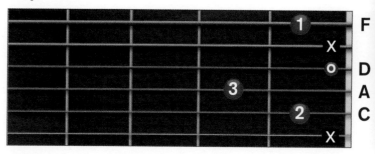

F
X
D
D A C
C
X

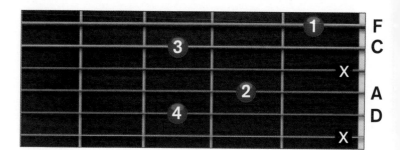

F
C
X
A
D
X

F Major 6ᵗʰ

Fret 3

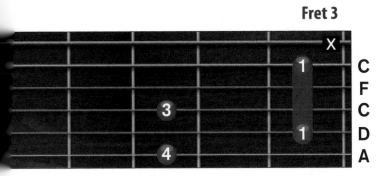

X
1 — C
F
3 — C
1 — D
4 — A

Fret 7

X
2 — F
3 — C
1 — D
4 — A
X

121

F Major 6th add 9th

1st position

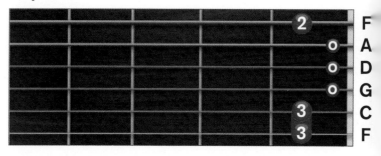

122

F Major 6th add 9th

Fret 7

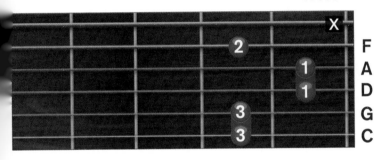

F
A
D
G
C

Fret 10

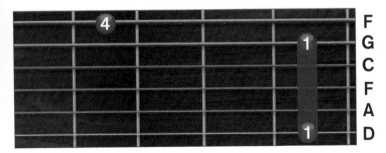

F
G
C
F
A
D

F Major 7th

1st position

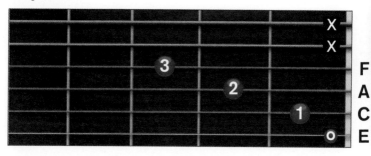

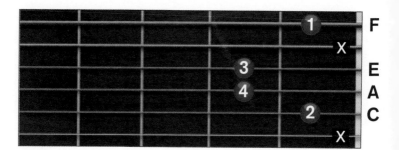

F Major 7th

Fret 3

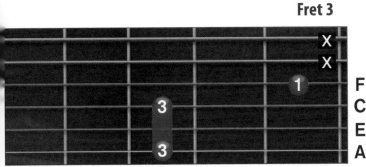

F
C
E
A

Fret 5

F
A
C
E
A

F Minor

1st position

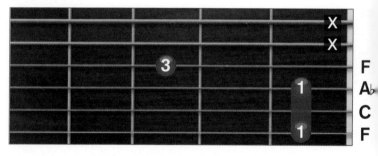

126

F Minor

Fret 4

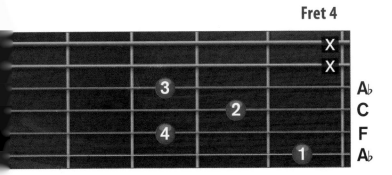

X
X
A♭
C
F
A♭

Fret 5

X
F
A♭
C
F
X

127

F Minor 6th

1st position

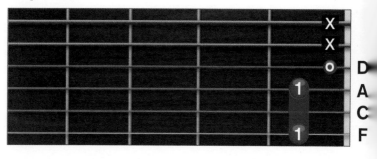

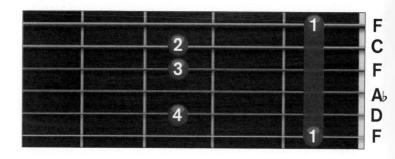

F Minor 6th

Fret 3

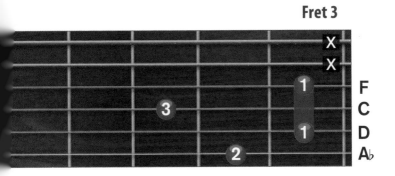

F
C
D
A♭

Fret 7

F

D
A♭
C

129

Fm7

F Minor 7th

1st position

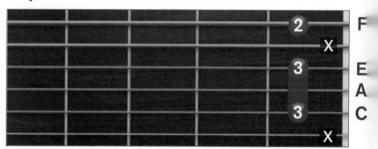

F
X
E
A
C
X

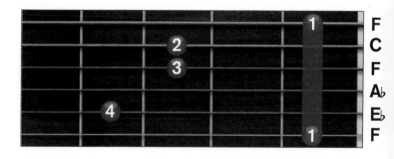

F
C
F
A♭
E♭
F

130

F Minor 7th

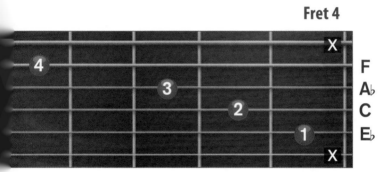

Fret 4

F
A♭
C
E♭

Fret 6

F
A♭
E♭
F
C

F Dominant 7th

1st position

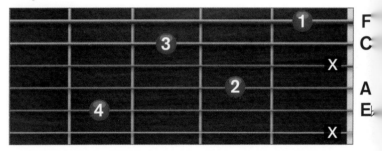

F
C
X
A
E♭
X

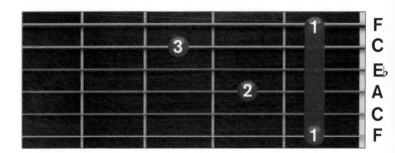

F
C
E♭
A
C
F

132

F Dominant 7th

Fret 3

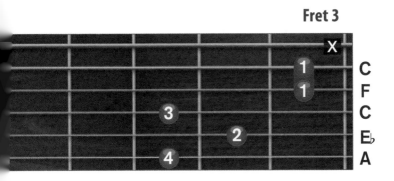

X
C
F
C
E♭
A

Fret 6

C
F
A
E♭
F
X

133

F Dominant 9th

1st position

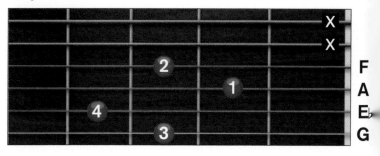

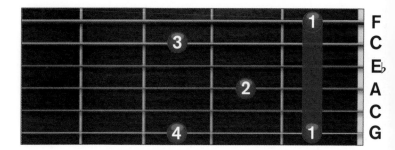

F Dominant 9th

Fret 5

F
E♭
E G A

Fret 7

F
A
E♭
G
C

F# Major

1st position

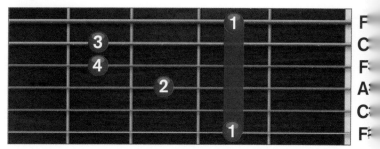

F
C
F#
A#
C#
F#

Fret 4

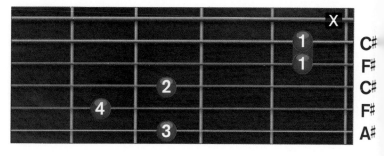

C#
F#
C#
F#
A#

F# Major

Fret 6

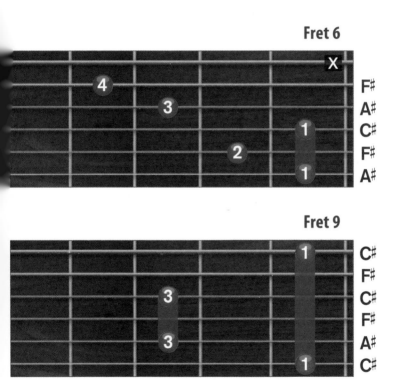

F#
A#
C#
F#
A#

Fret 9

C#
F#
C#
F#
A#
C#

F# Suspended 4th

1st position

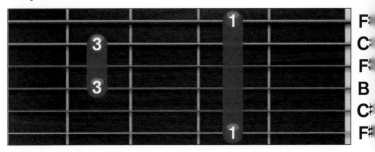

Fret 4

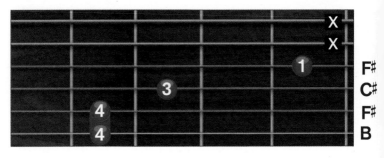

138

F# Suspended 4th

Fret 6

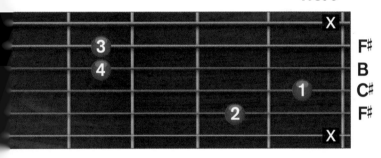

X
F#
B
C#
F#
X

Fret 6

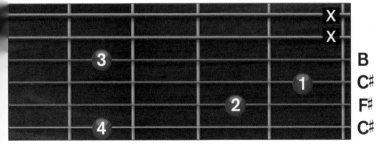

X
X
B
C#
F#
C#

F# Major 6th

1st position

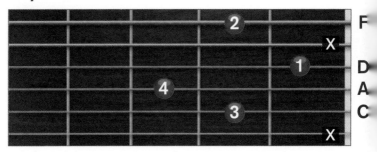

F# Major 6th

Fret 4

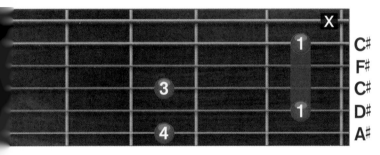

X
1 — C#
— F#
3 — C#
1 — D#
4 — A#

Fret 8

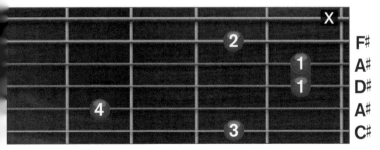

X
2 — F#
1 — A#
1 — D#
4 — A#
3 — C#

F# Major 6th add 9th

1st position

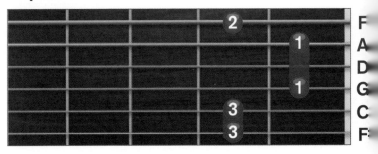

F
A
D
G
C
F

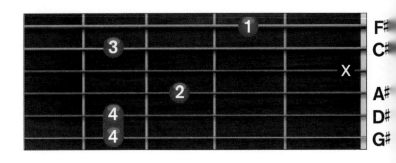

F#
C#
X
A#
D#
G#

142

F# Major 6th add 9th

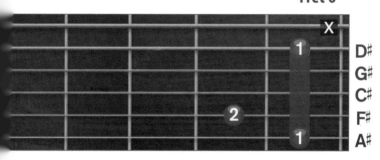

X
D#
G#
C#
F#
A#

X
F#
A#
D#
G#
C#

F# Major 7th

1st position

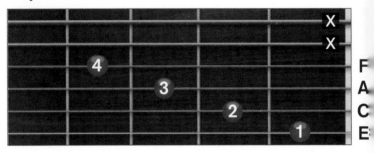

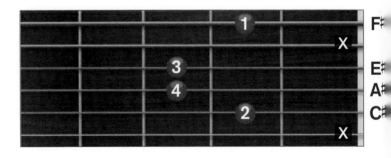

F# Major 7th

Fret 4

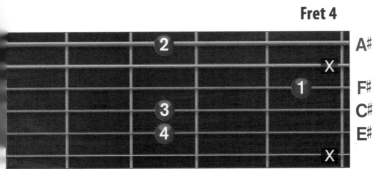

A#
X
F#
C#
E#
X

Fret 6

X
F#
A#
C#
E#
A#

145

F# Minor

1st position

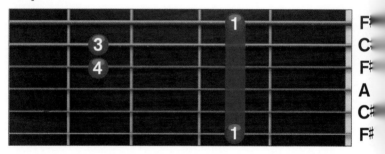

F#
C#
F#
A
C#
F#

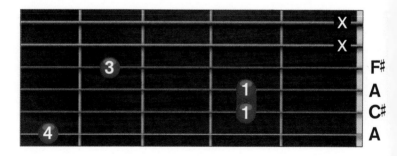

X
X
F#
A
C#
A

F# Minor

Fret 4

X
X
F#
C#
F#
A

Fret 6

X
F#
A
C#
F#
X

147

F# Minor 6th

1st position

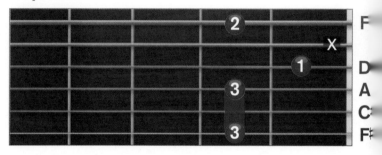

F
X
D
A
C#
F#

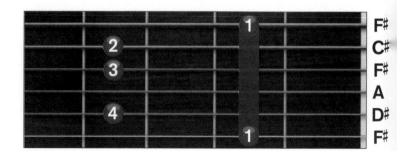

F#
C#
F#
A
D#
F#

148

F# Minor 6th

Fret 4

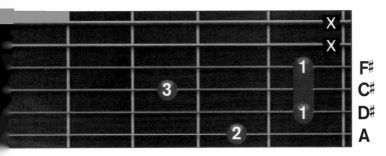

X
X
1 — F#
3
C#
1 — D#
2 — A

Fret 7

X
3 — F#
1 — A
2 — D#
1 — F#
4 — C#

149

F# Minor 7th

1st position

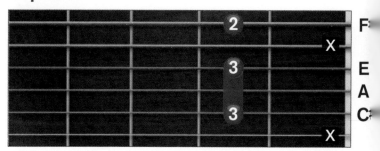

Fret 4

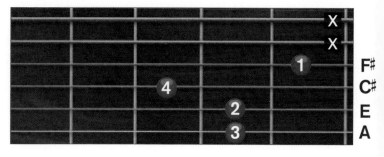

150

F♯ Minor 7th

Fret 7

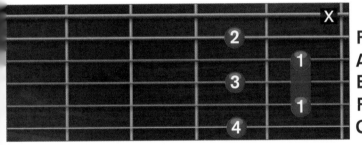

X
F♯
A
E
F♯
C♯

Fret 9

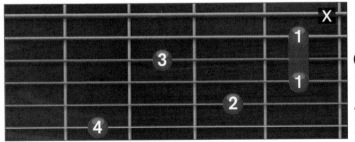

X
F♯
C♯
E
A
E

F# Dominant 7th

1st position

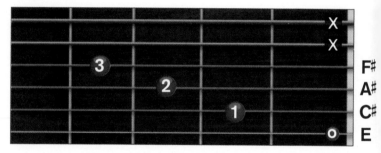

F#
A#
C#
E

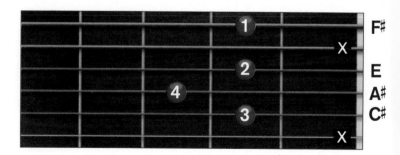

F#

E
A#
C#

F♯ Dominant 7th

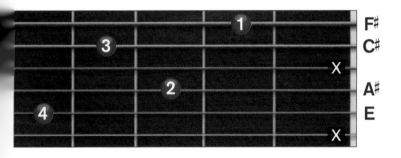

F# Dominant 9th

1st position

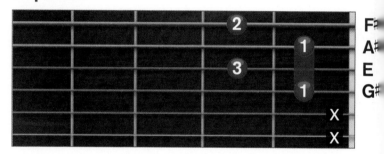

F#
A#
E
G#
X
X

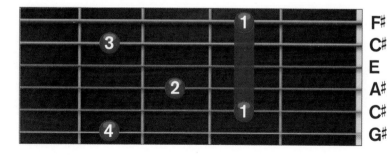

F#
C#
E
A#
C#
G#

F♯ Dominant 9th

Fret 3

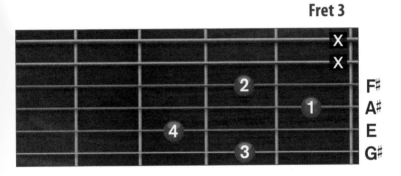

F♯
A♯
E
G♯

Fret 6

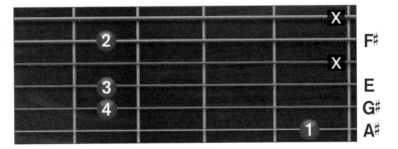

F♯
E
G♯
A♯

155

G Major

1st position

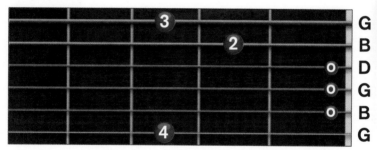

G
B
D
G
B
G

Fret 3

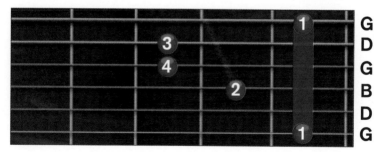

G
D
G
B
D
G

156

G Major

Fret 5

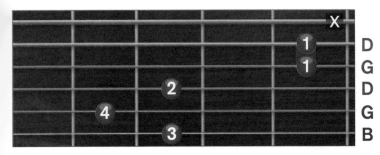

D
G
D
G
B

Fret 7

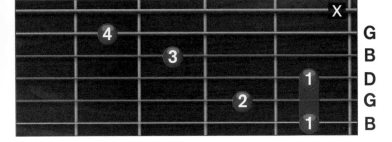

G
B
D
G
B

157

Gsus4

G Suspended 4th

1st position

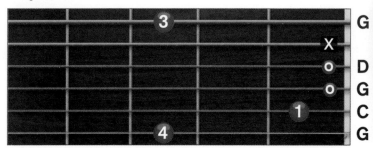

G
X
D
G
C
G

Fret 3

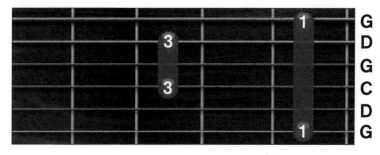

G
D
G
C
D
G

Gsus4

G Suspended 4th

Fret 5

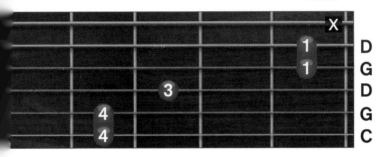

X
D
G
D
G
C

Fret 7

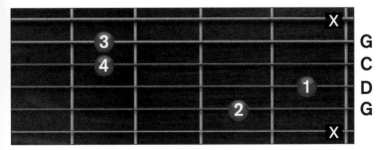

X
G
C
D
G
X

G Major 6th

1st position

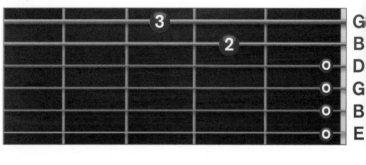

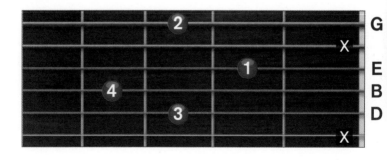

G Major 6ᵗʰ

X
X
G
B
D
E

Fret 3

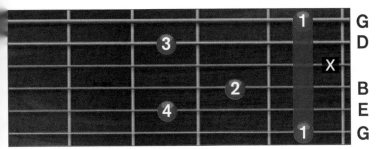

G
D
X
B
E
G

G Major 6th add 9th

1st position

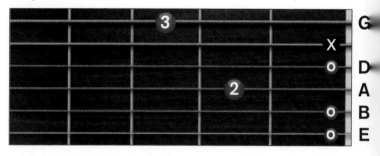

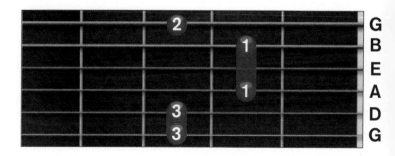

G Major 6th add 9th

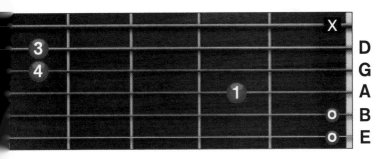

X

D
G
A
B
E

o
o

Fret 7

X

E
A
D
G
B

163

Gmaj7

G Major 7th

1st position

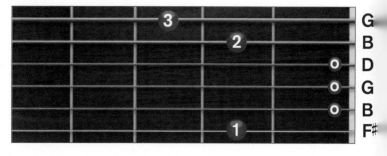

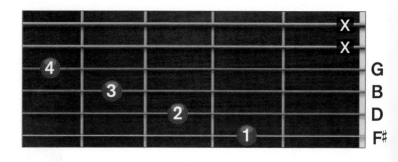

Gmaj7

G Major 7th

Fret 3

G
X
F#
B
D
X

Fret 5

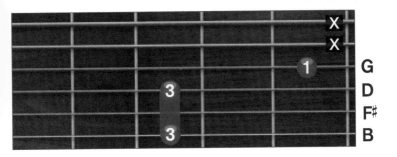

X
X
G
D
F#
B

G Minor

1st position

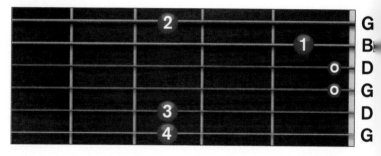

G
Bb
D
D
G
G

Fret 3

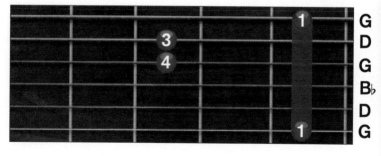

G
D
G
Bb
D
G

166

G Minor

Fret 3

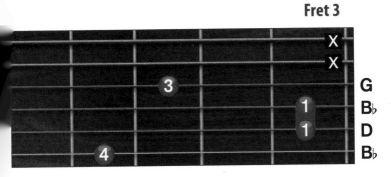

G
B♭
D
B♭

Fret 5

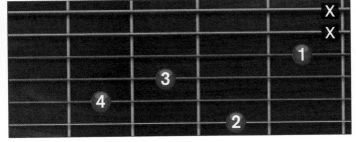

G
D
G
B♭

G Minor 6th

1st position

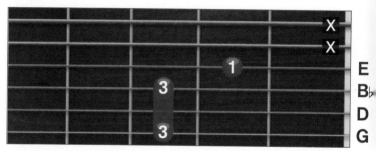

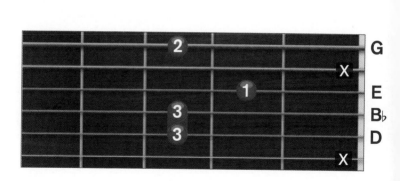

G Minor 6th

Fret 3

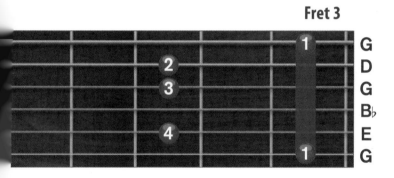

G
D
G
B♭
E
G

Fret 8

X
G
B♭
E
G
D

G Minor 7th

1st position

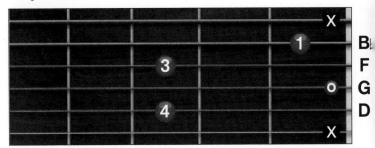

Bb
F
G
D

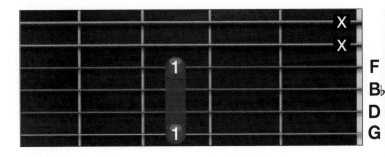

F
Bb
D
G

G Minor 7th

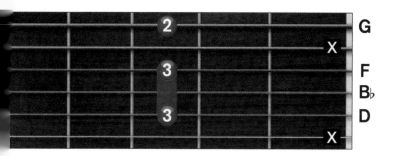

G
X
F
B♭
D
X

Fret 3

G
D
F
B♭
F
G

171

G Dominant 7th

1st position

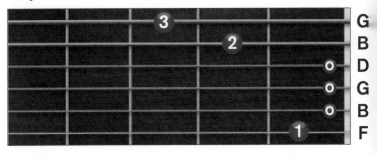

G Dominant 7th

Fret 3

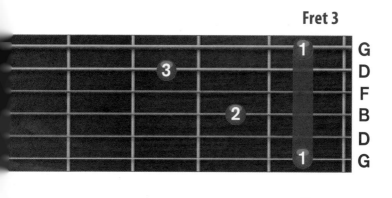

G
D
F
B
D
G

Fret 5

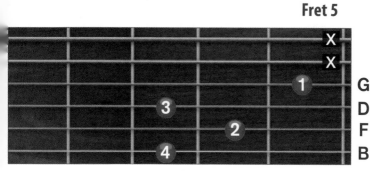

X
X
G
D
F
B

173

G Dominant 9th

1st position

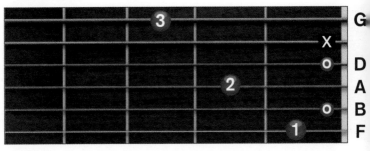

174

G Dominant 9th

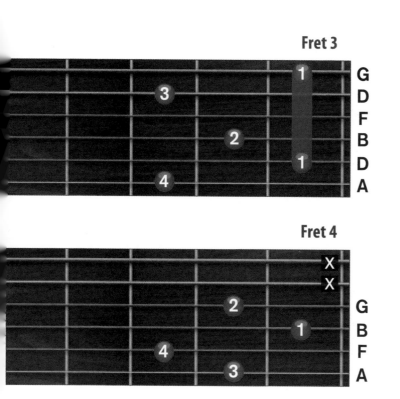

Fret 3

G
D
F
B
D
A

Fret 4

G
B
F
A

175

Ab Major

1st position

A
C
E
A
C
X

X
X
Eb
Ab
C
Ab

A♭ Major

Fret 4

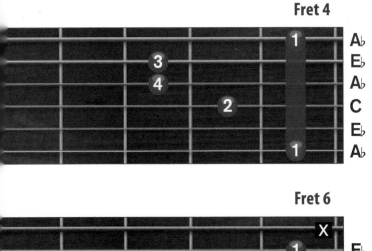

A♭
E♭
A♭
C
E♭
A♭

Fret 6

E♭
A♭
E♭
A♭
C

Absus4

A♭ Suspended 4th

1st position

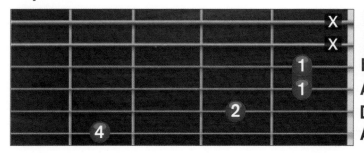

Fret 4

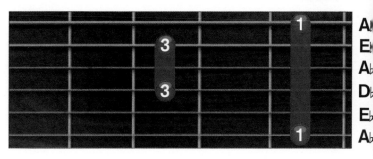

178

Absus4

A♭ Suspended 4th

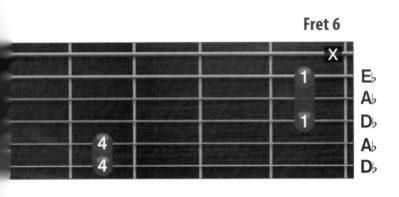

Fret 6

X
1 — E♭
— A♭
1 — D♭
4 — A♭
4 — D♭

Fret 8

X
3 — A♭
4 — D♭
1 — E♭
2 — A♭
X

179

Ab Major 6th

1st position

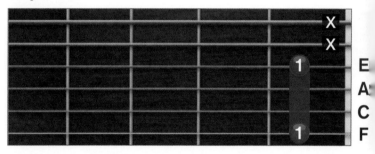

Fret 3

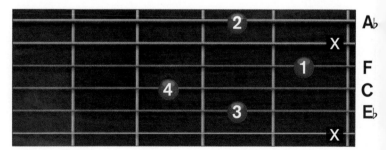

Ab Major 6th

Fret 4

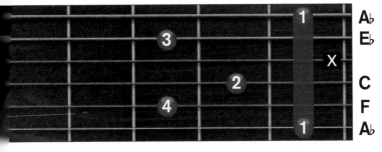

Ab
Eb
X
C
F
Ab

Fret 6

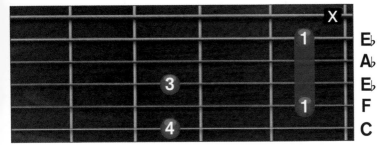

X
Eb
Ab
Eb
F
C

181

A♭ 6th add 9th

1st position

A♭
X
E♭
B♭
C
F

Fret 3

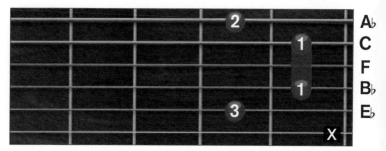

A♭
C
F
B♭
E♭
X

A♭ 6th add 9th

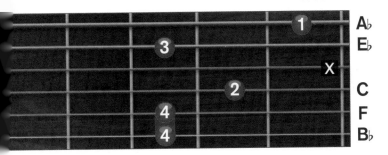

A♭
E♭
X
C
F
B♭

Fret 5

X
E♭
A♭
C
F
B♭

183

Abmaj7

A♭ Major 7th

1st position

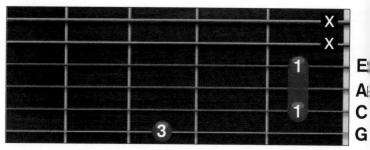

E♭
A♭
C
G

Fret 3

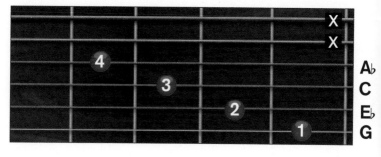

A♭
C
E♭
G

A♭ Major 7th

Fret 4

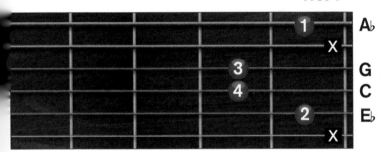

A♭
X
G
C
E♭
X

Fret 6

X
X
A♭
E♭
G
C

Ab Minor

1st position

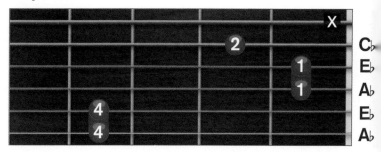

Cb
Eb
Ab
Eb
Ab

Fret 4

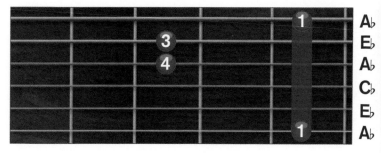

Ab
Eb
Ab
Cb
Eb
Ab

186

A♭ Minor

Fret 6

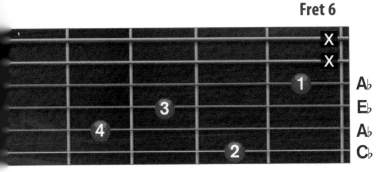

X
X
A♭
E♭
A♭
C♭

Fret 8

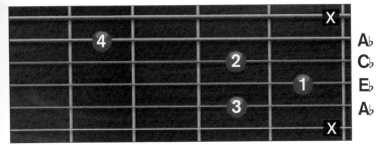

X
A♭
C♭
E♭
A♭
X

187

A♭ Minor 6th

1st position

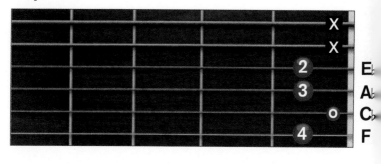

E♭
A♭
C♭
F

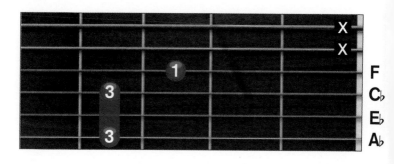

F
C♭
E♭
A♭

A♭ Minor 6th

Fret 4

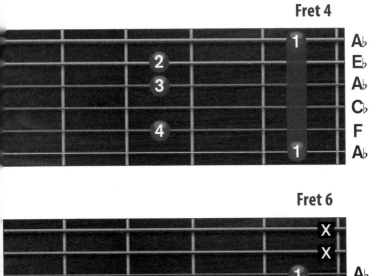

A♭
E♭
A♭
C♭
F
A♭

Fret 6

X
X
A♭
E♭
F
C♭

189

Abm7

Ab Minor 7th

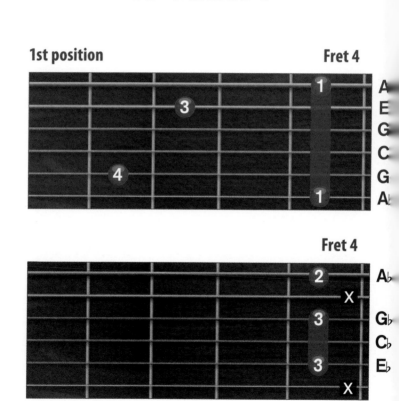

1st position

Fret 4

A
E
G
C
G
Ab

Fret 4

Ab
X
Gb
Cb
Eb
X

190

A♭ Minor 7th

Fret 6

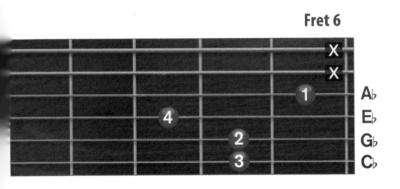

X
X
1   A♭
4   E♭
2   G♭
3   C♭

Fret 7

X
4   A♭
3   C♭
2   E♭
1   G♭
X

191

A♭ Dominant 7th

1st position

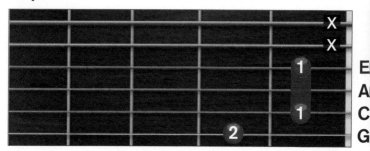

E
A♭
C
G♭

Fret 4

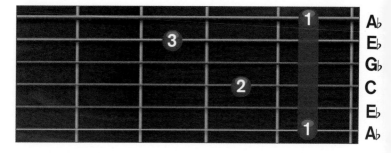

A♭
E♭
G♭
C
E♭
A♭

192

A♭ Dominant 7th

Fret 4

1 — A♭
X
2 — G♭
4 C
3 — E♭
X

Fret 6

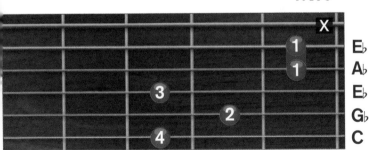

X
1 — E♭
1 — A♭
3 E♭
2 G♭
4 C

193

Ab Dominant 9th

1st position

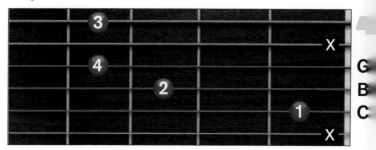

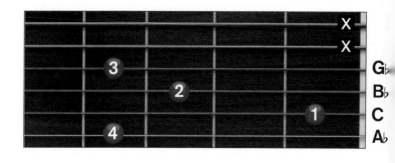

194

Ab Dominant 9th

Fret 4

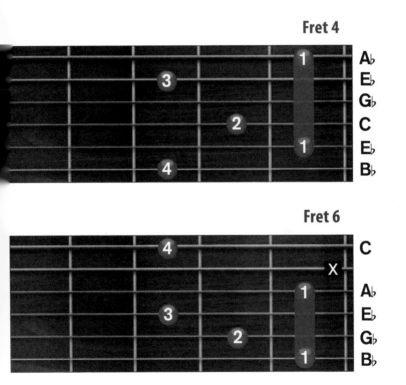

Ab
Eb
Gb
C
Eb
Bb

Fret 6

C
X
Ab
Eb
Gb
Bb

195

A Major

1st position

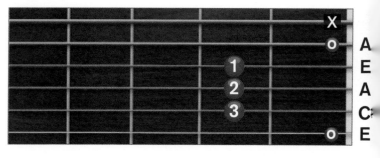

A
E
A
C#
E

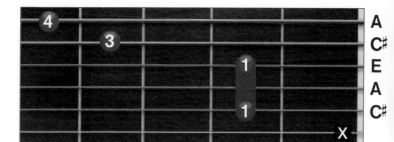

A
C#
E
A
C#

A Major

Fret 5

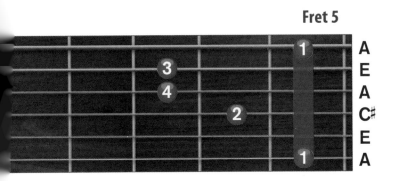

A
E
A
C#
E
A

Fret 7

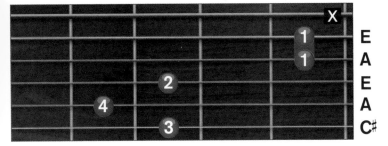

E
A
E
A
C#

Asus4

A Suspended 4th

1st position

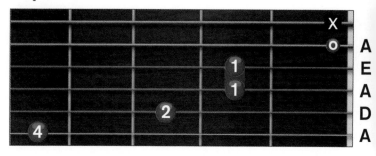

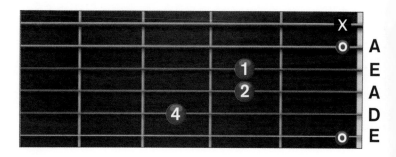

A Suspended 4th

Fret 5

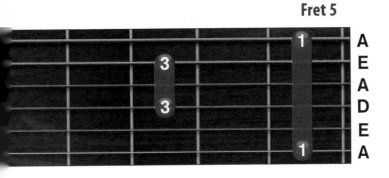

A
E
A
D
E
A

Fret 7

X
X
A
E
A
D

A Major 6th

1st position

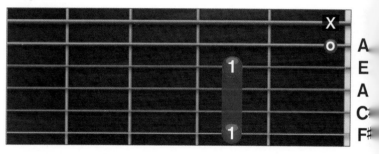

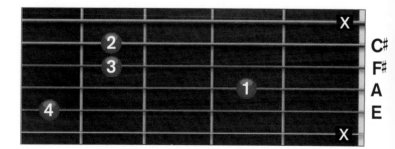

A Major 6th

Fret 4

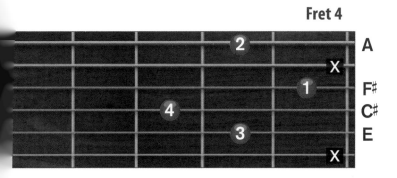

A
X
F#
C#
E
X

Fret 5

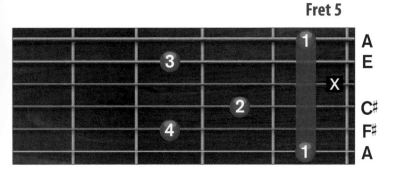

A
E
X
C#
F#
A

A Major 6th add 9th

1st position

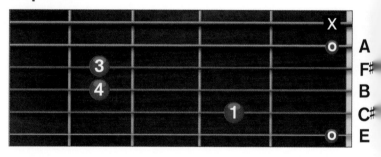

X
A
F#
B
C#
E

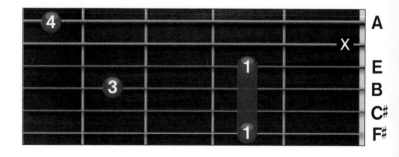

A
X
E
B
C#
F#

A Major 6th add 9th

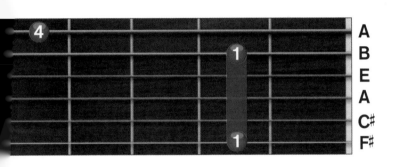

A
B
E
A
C#
F#

Fret 4

A
C#
F#
B
E
A

Amaj7

A Major 7th

1st position

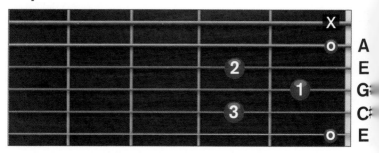

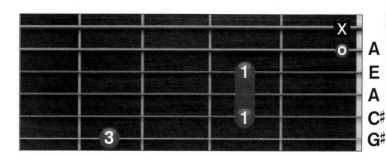

A Major 7th

Fret 4

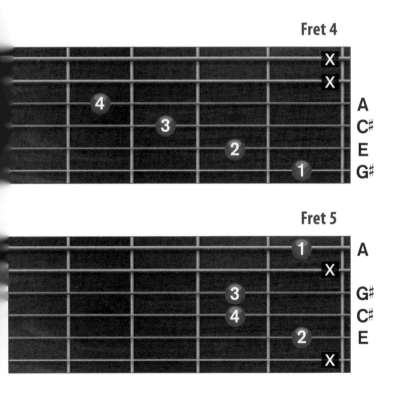

A
C#
E
G#

Fret 5

A

G#
C#
E

A Minor

1st position

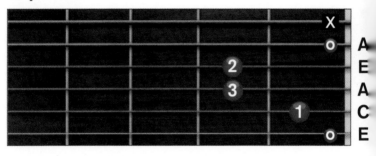

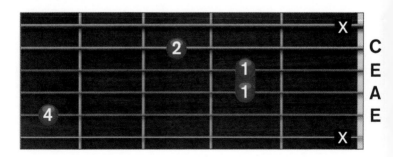

A Minor

Fret 5

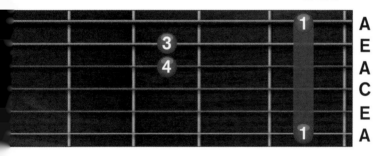

A
E
E
A
C
E
A

Fret 7

X
X
A
E
A
C

A Minor 6th

1st position

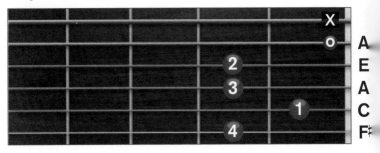

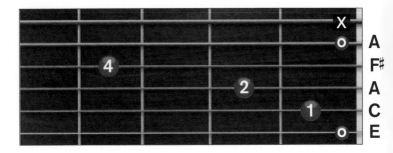

A Minor 6th

Fret 5

A
E
A
C
F#
A

Fret 7

X
X
A
E
F#
C

A Minor 7th

1st position

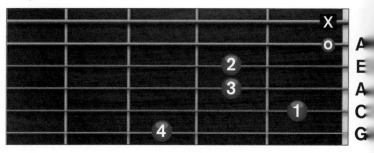

A
E
A
C
G

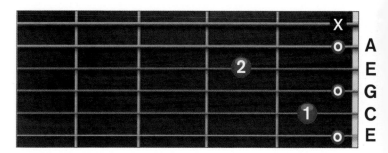

A
E
G
C
E

210

A Minor 7th

Fret 5

A
E
G
C
G
A

Fret 7

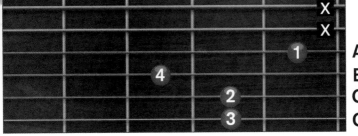

A
E
G
C

211

A Dominant 7th

1st position

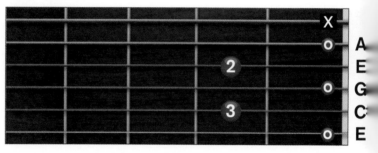

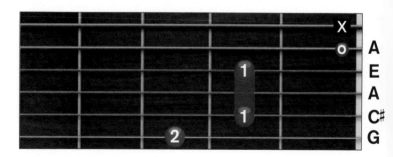

A Dominant 7th

Fret 5

A
E
G
C#
E
A

Fret 7

E
A
E
G
C#

213

A Dominant 9th

1st position

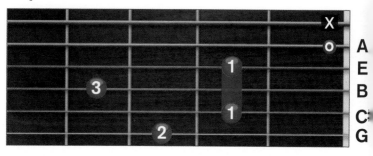

A Dominant 9th

Fret 4

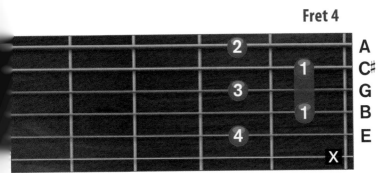

A
C#
G
B
E

Fret 5

A
E
G
C#
E
B

B♭ Major

1st position

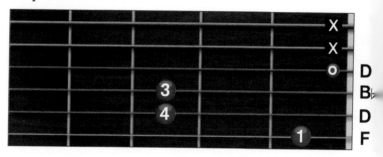

X
X
o   D
3   B♭
4   D
1   F

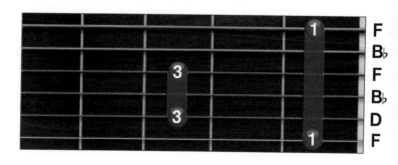

1   F
  B♭
3   F
3   B♭
  D
1   F

216

Bb Major

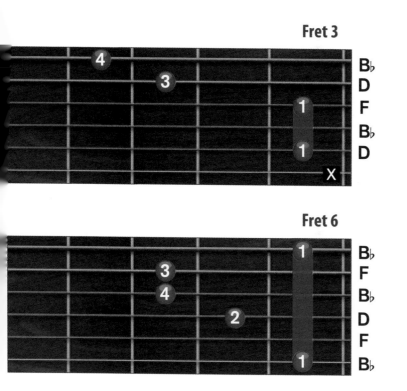

Fret 3

Bb
D
F
Bb
D
X

Fret 6

Bb
F
Bb
D
F
Bb

Bb Suspended 4th

1st position

F
Bb
Eb
F

F
Bb
Eb
Bb
Eb
F

Bb Suspended 4th

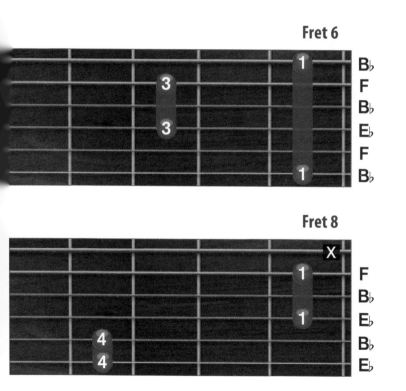

Fret 6

1 — Bb
3
F
3
Bb
3
Eb
F
1 — Bb

Fret 8

X
1 — F
Bb
1 — Eb
4
Bb
4
Eb

Bb Major 6th

1st position

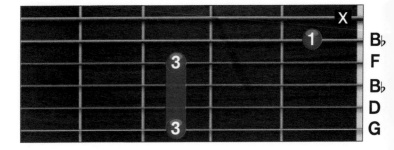

Bb Major 6th

Fret 3

Bb
D
F
Bb
D
G

Fret 5

Bb
X
G
D
F
X

B♭ 6th add 9th

1st position

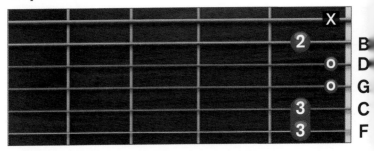

B
D
G
C
F

Fret 3

B♭
F
C
D
G

B♭ 6th add 9th

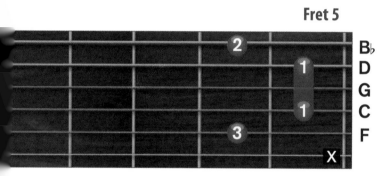

Fret 5

B♭
D
G
C
F
X

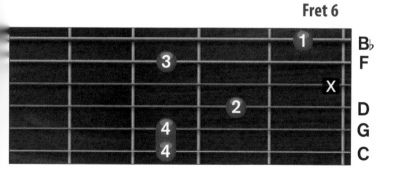

Fret 6

B♭
F
X
D
G
C

223

Bb Major 7th

1st position

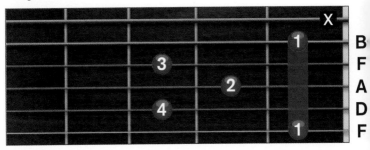

B♭ Major 7th

Fret 5

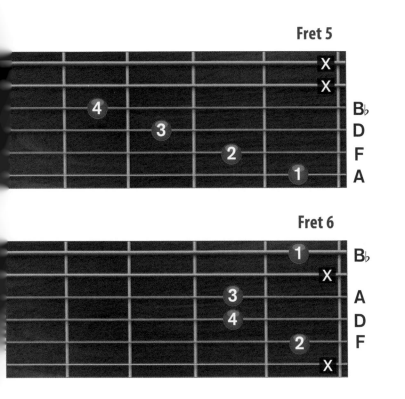

B♭
D
F
A

Fret 6

B♭

A
D
F

Bb Minor

1st position

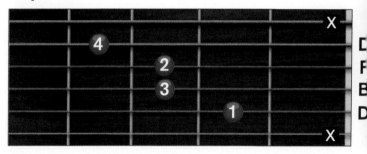

D
F
B
D
X

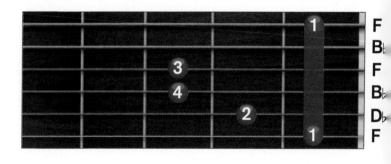

F
Bb
F
Bb
Db
F

Bbm

Bb Minor

Fret 3

F
Db
F
Bb

Fret 6

Bb
F
Bb
Db
F
Bb

Bbm6

Bb Minor 6th

1st position

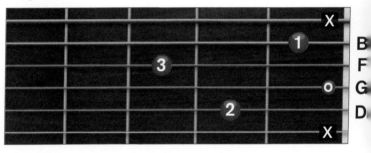

X
1 — B
3 — F
o — G
2 — D
X

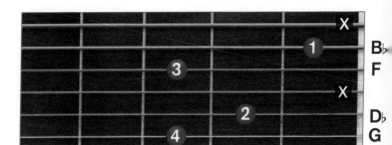

X
1 — Bb
3 — F
X
2 — Db
4 — G

Bbm6

Bb Minor 6th

Fret 5

Bb
X
G
Db
F
X

Fret 6

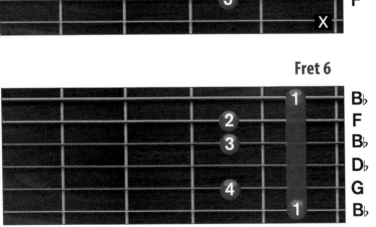

Bb
F
Bb
Db
G
Bb

229

B♭ Minor 7th

1st position

F
B
F
A♭
D♭
F

X
B♭
F
A♭
D♭
A♭

B♭ Minor 7th

Fret 6

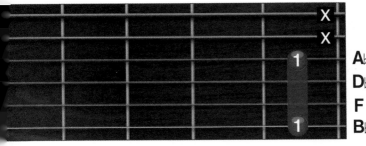

A♭
D♭
F
B♭

Fret 6

B♭
F
A♭
D♭
A♭
B♭

231

B♭ Dominant 7th

1st position

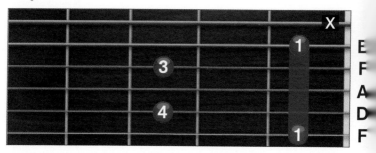

E
F
A
D
F

B♭
F
B♭
D
A♭

232

Bb Dominant 7th

Fret 6

Bb
F
Ab
D
F
Bb

Fret 8

X
F
Bb
F
Ab
D

Bb Dominant 9th

1st position

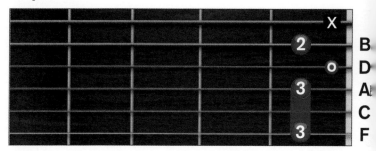

X
B
D
Ab
C
F

Fret 3

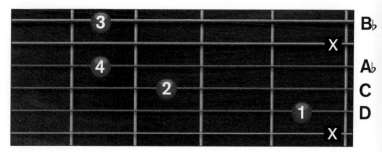

Bb
X
Ab
C
D
X

234

B♭ Dominant 9th

Fret 6

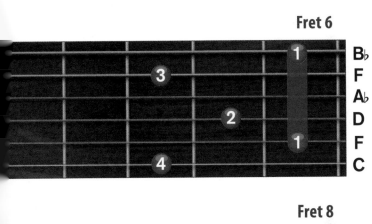

B♭
F
A♭
D
F
C

Fret 8

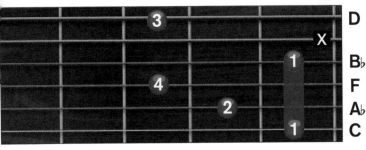

D
X
B♭
F
A♭
C

B Major

1st position

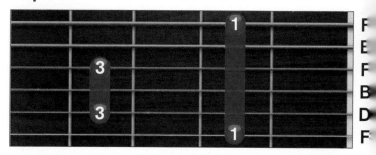

F
F
E
F
B
D
F

Fret 4

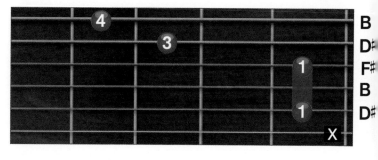

B
D#
F#
B
D#

B Major

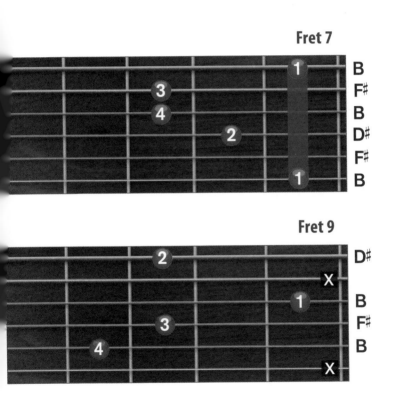

Fret 7

B
F#
B
D#
F#
B

Fret 9

D#
X
B
F#
B
X

237

B Suspended 4th

1st position

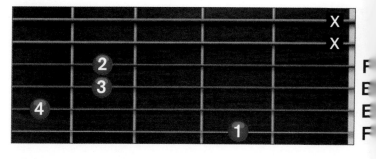

F
E
E
F

F#
B
E
B
E
F#

B Suspended 4th

Fret 7

B
F#
B
E
F#
B

Fret 7

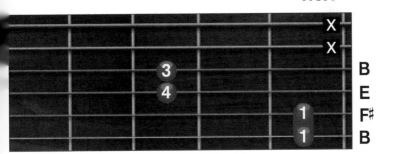

X
X
B
E
F#
B

B Major 6th

1st position

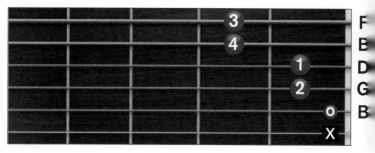

F
B
D
G
B
X

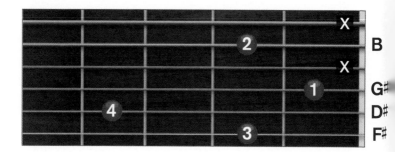

B

G#
D#
F#

B Major 6th

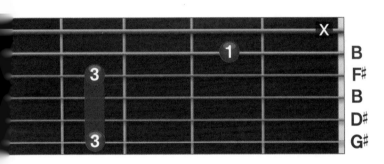

B
F#
B
D#
G#

Fret 6

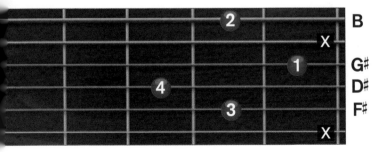

B

G#
D#
F#

B Major 6th add 9th

1st position

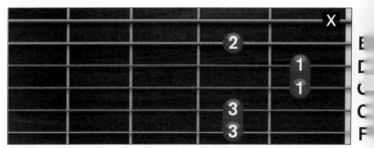

E
D
C
C
F

Fret 4

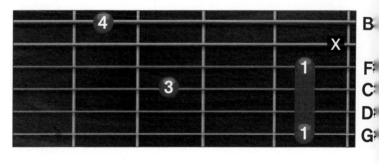

B

F
C
D
G

B Major 6th add 9th

Fret 6

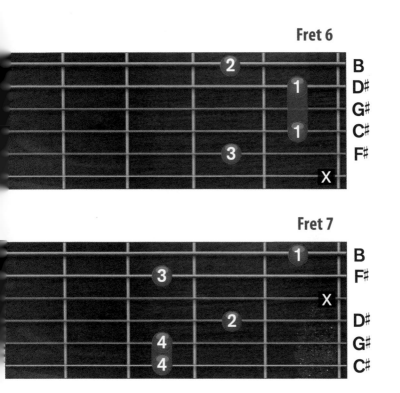

B
D#
G#
C#
F#
X

Fret 7

B
F#
X
D#
G#
C#

243

B Major 7th

1st position

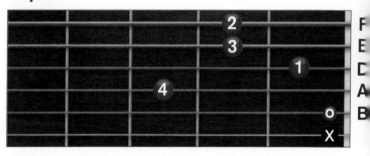

F
E
D
A
B
B

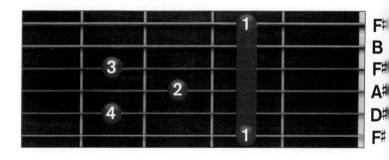

F#
B
F#
A#
D#
F#

244

Bmaj7
B Major 7th

Fret 4

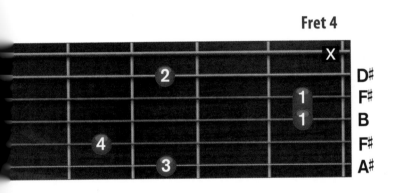

X
D#
F#
B
F#
A#

Fret 6

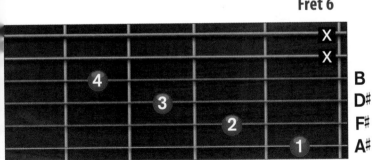

X
X
B
D#
F#
A#

245

B Minor

1st position

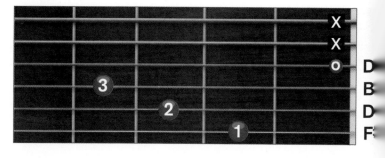

X
X
o   D
    B
    D
    F#

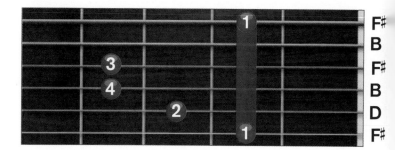

F#
B
F#
B
D
F#

B Minor

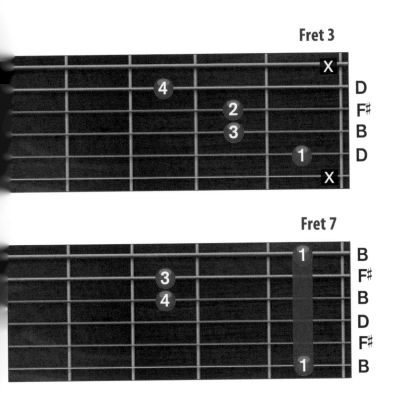

Fret 3

X
D
F#
B
D
X

Fret 7

B
F#
B
D
F#
B

B Minor 6th

1st position

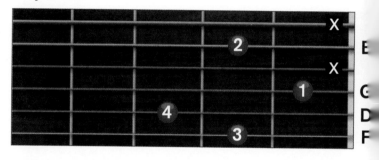

E
G
D
F

B
F#
G#
D

248

B Minor 6th

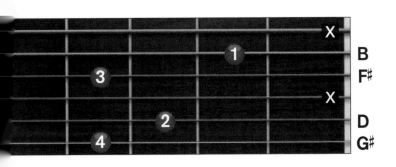

X
B
F#
X
D
G#

Fret 6

B
X
G#
D
F#
B

B Minor 7th

1st position

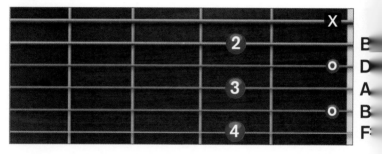

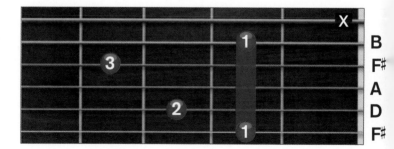

Bm7

B Minor 7th

Fret 3

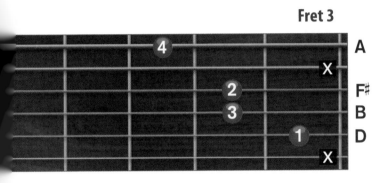

A
X
F#
B
D
X

Fret 7

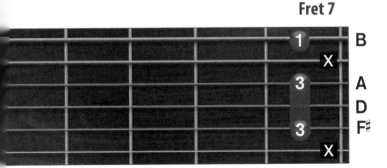

B
X
A
D
F#
X

B Dominant 7th

1st position

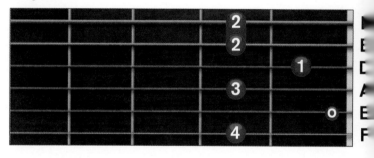

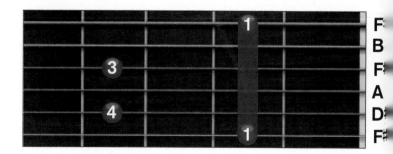

B Dominant 7th

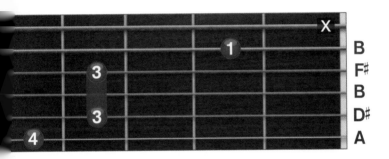

B
F#
B
D#
A

Fret 7

B
F#
A
D#
F#
B

B Dominant 9th

1st position

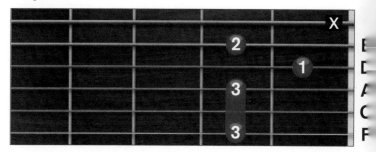

E
D
A
C
F

Fret 4

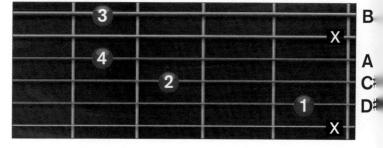

B
A
C#
D#

254

B Dominant 9th

Fret 6

B
D#
A
C#
X
X

Fret 7

B
F#
A
D#
F#
C#

255

TOOLS OF THE TRADE

Capos are great devices—by simply attaching them to any fret on the fretboard you can change the keys of the open chord shapes you've learned. This option is useful when you play with musicians who play in unusual keys. There are different styles of capos to choose from. What's important is to choose the one with which you're most comfortable.

All guitar cables are not made the same. They can get expensive, so determine your budget first. Select one that aligns comfortably with the orientation of your guitar's input jac Will you be moving around while yo play? Some cables flop pliantly on the floor, while others tend to curl u in rigid loops. You may want to look at the cables used by guitarists who play in the style you want to play.

If you plan on playing while standing up, a guitar strap is a necessity. Besides being durable and comfortable, your strap should fit securely over both strap attachments on your guitar.

There are hundreds of guitar tuners to choose from. Although tuning by ear is a good way to develop a sense of pitch, there's nothing wrong with having one of these little devices around to help you get your guitar perfectly tuned.